MILLIC
MANTRA: HOW TO
BE MILLIONAIRE

GW01319647

ARVIND UPADHYAY

Copyright © Arvind Upadhyay
All Rights Reserved.

ISBN 979-888569727-9

This book has been published with all efforts taken to make the material error-free after the consent of the author. However, the author and the publisher do not assume and hereby disclaim any liability to any party for any loss, damage, or disruption caused by errors or omissions, whether such errors or omissions result from negligence, accident, or any other cause.

While every effort has been made to avoid any mistake or omission, this publication is being sold on the condition and understanding that neither the author nor the publishers or printers would be liable in any manner to any person by reason of any mistake or omission in this publication or for any action taken or omitted to be taken or advice rendered or accepted on the basis of this work. For any defect in printing or binding the publishers will be liable only to replace the defective copy by another copy of this work then available.

We live in a world of duality: up and down, light and dark, hot and cold, in and out, fast and slow, right and left. These are but a few examples of the thousands of opposite poles. For one pole to exist, the other pole must also exist. Is it possible to have a right side without a left side? Not a chance. Consequently, just as there are "outer" laws of money, there must be "inner" laws. The outer laws include things like business knowledge, money management, and investment strategies. These are essential. But the inner game is just as important. An analogy would be a carpenter and his tools. Having top-of-the-line tools is imperative, but being the topnotch carpenter who masterfully uses those tools is even more critical. I have a saying: "It's not enough to be in the right place at the right time. You have to be the right person in the right place at the right time." So who are you? How do you think? What are your beliefs? What are your habits and traits? How do you really feel about yourself ? How confident are you in yourself ? How well do you relate to others? How much do you trust others? Do you truly feel that you deserve wealth? What is your ability to act in spite of fear, in spite of worry, in spite of inconvenience, in spite of discomfort? Can you act when you're not in the mood? The fact is that your character, your thinking, and your beliefs are a critical part of what determines the level of your success. One of my favorite authors, Stuart Wilde, puts it this way: "The key to success is to raise your own energy; when you do, people will naturally be attracted to you. And when they show up, bill 'em!" WEALTH PRINCIPLE: Your income can grow only to the extent you do! Why Is Your Money Blueprint Important? Have you heard of people who have "blown up" financially? Have you noticed how some people have a lot of money and then lose it, or have excellent opportunities start well but then go sour on them? Now you know the real cause. On the outside it looks like bad luck, a downturn in the economy, a lousy partner, whatever. On the inside, however, it's another matter. That's why, if you come into big money when you're not ready for it on the inside, the chances are your wealth will be short-lived and you will lose it. The vast majority of people simply do not have the internal capacity to create and hold on to large amounts of money and the increased challenges that go with more money and success. That, my friends, is the primary reason they don't have much money. A perfect example is lottery winners. Research has shown again and again that regardless of the size of their winnings, most lottery winners eventually return to their original financial state, the amount they can comfortably handle. On the other hand, the opposite occurs for self-made millionaires. Notice that when self-made millionaires lose their money, they usually have it back within a relatively short time. Donald Trump is a good example. Trump was worth billions, lost everything, and then a couple of years later, got it all back again and more. Why does this phenomenon occur? Because even though some self-made millionaires may lose their money, they never lose the most important ingredient to their success: their millionaire mind. Of course in "The Donald" 's case, it's his "billionaire" mind. Do you realize Donald Trump could never be just a millionaire? If Donald Trump had a net worth of only 1 million dollars, how do you think he'd feel about his financial success? Most people would agree that he'd probably feel broke, like a financial failure! That's because Donald Trump's financial "thermostat" is set for billions, not millions. Most people's financial thermostats are set for generating thousands, not millions of dollars; some people's financial thermostats are set for generating hundreds, not even thousands; and some people's financial thermostats are set for below zero. They're frickin' freezing and they don't have a clue as to why! The reality is that most people do not reach their full potential. Most people are not successful. Research shows that 80 percent of individuals will never be financially free in the way they'd like to be, and 80 percent will never claim to be truly happy. The reason is simple. Most people are unconscious. They are a little asleep at the wheel. They work and think on a superficial level of life—based only on what they can see. They live strictly in the visible world. The Roots Create the Fruits Imagine a tree. Let's suppose this tree represents the tree of life. On this tree there are fruits. In life, our fruits are called our results. So we look at the fruits (our results) and we don't like them; there aren't enough of them, they're too small, or they don't taste good. So what do we tend to do? Most of us put even more attention and focus on the fruits, our results. But what is it that actually creates those particular fruits? It's the seeds and the roots that create those fruits. It's what's under the ground that creates what's above the ground. It's what's invisible that creates what's visible. So what does that mean? It means that if you want to change the fruits, you will first have to change the roots. If you want to change the visible, you must first change the invisible.

WEALTH PRINCIPLE:

If you want to change the fruits, you will first have to change the roots. If you want to change the visible, you must first change the invisible.

Of course, some say that seeing is believing. The question I have for such people is "Why do you bother paying your electric bill?" Although you cannot see electricity, you can certainly recognize and use its power. If you have any doubt as to whether it exists, just stick your finger in an electric socket, and I guarantee that your doubts will quickly disappear. In my experience, what you cannot see in this world is far more powerful than anything you can see. You may or may not agree with this statement, but to the extent that you do not apply this principle in your life, you must be suffering. Why? Because you are going against the laws of nature, whereby what is under the ground creates what is above the ground, where what is invisible creates what is visible. As humans, we are a part of nature, not above it. Consequently, when we align with the laws of nature and work on our roots—our "inner" world—our life flows smoothly. When we don't, life gets rough. In every forest, on every farm, in every orchard on earth, it's what's under the ground that creates what's above the ground. That's why placing your attention on the fruits that you have already grown is futile. You cannot change the fruits that are already hanging on the tree. You can, however, change tomorrow's fruits. But to do so, you will have to dig below the ground and strengthen the roots.

One of the most important things you can ever understand is that we do not live on only one plane of existence. We live in at least four different realms at once. These four quadrants are the physical world, the mental world, the emotional world, and the spiritual world. What most people never realize is that the physical realm is merely a "printout" of the other three. For example, let's suppose you've just written a letter on your computer. You hit the print key and the letter comes out of your printer. You look at your hard copy, and lo and behold, you find a typo. So you take out your trusty eraser and rub out the typo. Then you hit print again and out comes the same typo. Oh my gosh, how could this be? You just erased it! So this time you get a bigger eraser and you rub even harder and longer. You even study a three-hundred-page manual called Effective Erasing. Now you've got all the "tools" and knowledge you need. You're ready. You hit print and there it is again! "No way!" you cry out, stunned in amazement. "How could this be? What's going on here? Am I in the twilight zone?" What's going on here is that the real problem cannot be changed in the "printout," the physical world; it can only be changed in the "program," the mental, emotional, and spiritual worlds. Money is a result, wealth is a result, health is a result, illness is a result, your weight is a result. We live in a world of cause and effect.

WEALTH PRINCIPLE:

Money is a result, wealth is a result, health is a result, illness is a result, your weight is a result. We live in a world of cause and effect.

Have you ever heard someone assert that a lack of money was a bit of a problem? Now hear this: A lack of money is never, ever, ever a problem. A lack of money is merely a symptom of what is going on underneath. Lack of money is the effect, but what is the root cause? It boils down to this. The only way to change your "outer" world is to first change your "inner" world. Whatever results you're getting, be they rich or poor, good or bad, positive or negative, always remember that your outer world is simply a reflection of your inner world. If things aren't going well in your outer life, it's because things aren't going well in your inner life. It's that simple.

next time next year we will be Millionaires

Contents

Contents

Foreword

You have to believe you can be successful before you will ever succeed. Sounds like a cliché, doesn't it? But take time to stop and think about it. Where else can you begin? Your beliefs create your life experience -- it's not the other way around. And no matter what you believed before, you can change your beliefs and change your life. It's impossible to create success without believing -- deeply -- that you are capable of being successful. It's impossible to live abundantly without believing that you deserve abundance. Our education, society, and other forms of mental conditioning are all, unfortunately, more pessimistic than optimistic. How often has someone told you not to waste your time on pipe dreams, that you have to be realistic, that you can't have what you want? Because we hear this so often and, as a result, believe it to be true, wealth always seems reserved for the fortunate few. Success seems an exclusive party to which we are cordially not invited. But this is simply not true. If success and prosperity are an exclusive club, it's because they are so in the minds of people whose attitudes bar their own entry. Every successful person at some point came to believe that one day he or she would be successful. Your beliefs about success are, no doubt, deeply ingrained, and you have to be open to changing them before you'll ever succeed. Examine your beliefs to see how they have affected your life. Many people needlessly sabotage themselves because of unexamined "core beliefs" about how the world operates. Marc Allen sums it up in Visionary Business : It's important -- in some cases critically important -- to regularly take time to examine our lives. The first thing to do is to take a look at our past -- as clearly and honestly as we can -- and discover the important events and influences that have shaped our lives.... Some of these shaping events have led to very good core beliefs -- and those moments should be remembered, and those beliefs should be encouraged and supported. All of us have had someone in our lives who saw our potential and supported us in one way or another. We've all had glimpses of our genius, as children, and we 've all had other forces that have sought to crush our genius, through doubt, through cynicism, through lack of faith. We need to reflect on these things occasionally. Those shaping moments that have had a negative impact on us need to be looked at, and we need to discover the negative core beliefs we formed as a result. Once those beliefs are identified, they can be let go of. Because they aren't true -- they're simply self-fulfilling things that become true if we believe them. This is the process of becoming conscious -- becoming aware of the forces that drive us, and learning how to act on those forces, how to shape our destiny, how to become powerful. How to achieve what we want in life. What are your beliefs about success? Don't be afraid to analyze your thoughts more closely; you may be surprised at the barriers you have put between yourself and success, once you think about it. When you realize that you can change even your most deeply held beliefs, you can come to see that not only is it possible for you to become as successful as you would like -- in all areas of your life -- but also that it's easy, much easier than you have ever dreamed possible. In fact, dozens of opportunities appear to you every day. Profitable ideas flash through your mind, but you usually let them slip away without pursuing them with concrete action. The art of self-suggestion, which is discussed throughout this book, helps you discover how to develop your powers of intuition -- the sixth sense for success. You already have these qualities, but you may not be fully aware of their existence. You only need to access them -- and you can, quite easily. SUCCEEDING IS NO HARDER THAN FAILING For most people, failure has become a way of life. Failure is a hard habit to break; after all, our social climate has given us high expectations, but our social conditioning has given us low morale. It's a vicious cycle. In order to become successful, we have to understand that success is basically no more difficult than failure . It's simply based on a different kind of mental programming, one to which the subconscious mind is not inherently opposed. Doesn't every failure involve a highly complex combination of circumstances? Consider what it takes to miss perfect opportunities, to misfire every time you attempt something, to avoid meeting the people who can help you on your path of success, to dismiss your ideas as useless when they could lead to something worthwhile, and to continually repeat the motions that lead to defeat. It's quite an achievement to fail, and yet the subconscious mind accepts defeat as natural. Throughout this book, we analyze the vital role the subconscious plays in manifesting success. When we understand how to get the power of our subconscious mind working on success rather than failure, we will succeed. It is inevitable. We create all sorts of excuses to block our success. How many of these thoughts creep into your mind? * Everything was much easier in the good old days. This excuse is proven wrong every single day of the year. While negative, shortsighted people drone on about unemployment, downsizing, and outsourcing, thousands of small businesses start and flourish every year. Thousands -- globally, millions -- of people become millionaires each year! Think of the movies produced, the books published, the new opportunities in computer science and Internet media! Think of the parts of the world that are opening to free trade! Becoming successful is not only possible today; it's actually easier than it used to be. The entire world is ours to offer our new ideas, products, services -- whatever gift we have to give. Success depends far less on outside circumstances than on our mental attitude, our beliefs about ourselves and the world. *I'm too young. Tell this to Debbie Fields, founder and owner of Mrs. Fields Cookies, who was in her twenties when she achieved success, or Steve Jobs, founder of Apple Computers, who made his first million when he was twenty-three, his first ten million at twenty-four, and his first hundred million at twentyfive. There is an old saying: "A youth with a single aim in life arrives early at the harvest." Youth is more often than not an asset. Lack of experience can be compensated for by boldness, daring, instinct, and originality. History shows that most successful people started out completely inexperienced and learned as they went along. * I'm too old. Colonel Sanders and Georgia O'Keeffe would disagree. Napoleon Hill's survey of the wealthy showed that many successful people don't reach their goals until midlife and beyond. It could be that this is the time of reaping the benefits of a series of earlier efforts, while many others are thinking of retirement. Work does not kill. Idleness, on the other hand, is often deadly; people who take early retirement often die younger than those who keep working. The fact remains that many people begin a second or third career, sometimes the most successful of all, late in life. Age is irrelevant. Your years of experience, even if you have failed, are priceless to you. * I have no capital. Most people don't, in the beginning. Money isn't essential when we start out. A good creative idea or business idea and a positive mental outlook are essential. Everyone in the world has at least one talent, one passion, one hobby that can become profitable if applied correctly. Contrary to popular belief, there is no shortage of money in the world. The money for launching ideas and furthering good in our world is always available. Poverty seems to be a tradition in far too many families, an inherited trait like the color of one's hair or eyes, passed down from generation to generation. It's often more difficult for people whose families have always been poor to imagine that one day they can become rich. The image we get of ourselves and of life in general is often tinged with hopelessness and pessimism, and the role models that surround us are not always very inspiring. But there are so many exceptions to this -- look at Charlie Chaplin, for example, one of history's wealthiest actors. He spent his youth in poverty, wandering the streets of London. The humiliation of poverty and early contact with life's harsh realities have in many cases spurred people on to great achievement. * I'm not educated. Thomas Edison left school before the age of sixteen. Microsoft's Bill Gates is a college dropout. Even though many successful people weren't educated in the formal sense, they did acquire an indepth knowledge of the industry in which they made their fortunes. * I don't have any special talent. Many successful people displayed no early signs of being destined for fame, fortune, and fulfillment. J. Paul Getty said, "I most certainly was not a born businessman." Many people talk themselves into believing that they don't have an inborn talent or what it takes to change their lives. They go to great lengths to justify their lack of success. But in reality, everyone in the world has some talent, some kind of gift. Once we discover our own unique gift, it becomes our purpose to develop it, and doing so leads to our success. * I don't have the energy it takes. There is often an important difference between those who succeed and those who fail: their levels of energy. Every action we take requires a minimum amount of energy, especially mental or psychic energy. Low vitality inevitably breeds low motivation. This appears to be another inescapable vicious cycle. But all it takes is a tiny spark to ignite the resources of energy that lie dormant within us. The potential energy we all have is enormous. In many people, it is hibernating, waiting to be activated. Yet at the same time, it takes much more energy to do something we don't like than something we enjoy. Think of the energy you have and how time slips away when you're absorbed in your favorite project. When we do what truly interests and motivates us, the energy flows easily and effortlessly. * I'm afraid of failure. We're born with two fears: falling and loud noises. All other fears are acquired. Unfortunately, the fear of failure is powerful and widespread -- and it is paralyzing. Often deeply embedded within us, it results from past failures, from a lack of confidence bred unknowingly by our parents, and it's enforced by society's general negative, short-sighted thinking. The fear of failure is sometimes expressed overtly but is most often unconscious and subtly disguised. People don't admit they're afraid of failing; instead, they denigrate others for building castles in the air, and they scorn dreams and creative ideas. They're champion excuse-makers: family obligations, problems, lack of time, lack of money. But wouldn't the family prefer a spouse or parent who is content with his or her work? Wouldn't time be better spent in creative expression? Wouldn't creating fulfillment resolve many problems? Then there are the "if only" people: If only their boss would notice them. . . . If only they could come up with a good idea. . . . If only they had more talent, ability, time, money, or luck. . . . If only they had been born in different circumstances, or under another astrological sign. . . . Obviously, if you never try anything, chances are you will never fail. But then, you're not likely to succeed either. Success doesn't miraculously appear out of the blue. It's always the result of concrete action and a positive mental attitude. Thomas Edison made hundreds -- some say thousands -- of attempts before perfecting the incandescent lightbulb. Abraham Lincoln lost eighteen elections before becoming president of the United States. We're not singing the praises of failure, but we know through experience that every personal defeat can be an education in itself, at least if it's accepted with an open mind. * All I've done is fail. One underlying reason for many people's paralyzing fear of failure is that they have already failed, or at least believe they were unsuccessful in the past. Each new setback reinforces this feeling and undermines their self-confidence. People start with one failure and see themselves as losers, and this in turn leads inevitably to more aborted attempts. These failures reinforce their loser mentality, and soon it becomes habitual. They end up believing that life is a series of hard knocks, defeats, struggles, and frustrations. Why have you failed until now? Maybe you wanted to fail -- at least on some level, possibly subconsciously. If the success you're entitled to always slips through your fingers, ask yourself why you've condemned yourself to mediocrity. And reassure yourself that even the strongest, most powerful negative programming can be changed -- quickly and completely. Once you examine it closely, you may be surprised at your inner resistance to success. You may be surprised at your negative inner monologue, which most people relentlessly repeat out of habit. Here's an important point: Your mind is always working for your welfare -- it just may be working for a long outmoded goal. For instance, maybe your high energy or enthusiasm for something as a child brought harsh criticism from your parents or siblings. You very quickly learned to be quiet and restrained. But now, as an adult, there's no reason to remain unseen and unheard -- yet no one told your subconscious mind. Look at it this way: Our failures should be seen as stepping-stones that bring us closer to our goal. Our failures give us tremendous feedback. Isn't it true that with each perceived failure we learn something of value? Failure is our way of learning and growing. In reality, there is no such thing as failure: It's just part of our education on the way to our inevitable success -- if we look at it that way. Your situation will not improve if you do nothing about it. Of course, this is obvious. But then why are so many people waiting for their big break, or to win the lottery, or for some other miracle? Most people live with the idea that everything will magically work out. And then comes disappointment. Success isn't handed to us on a silver platter; we have to take action, we have to challenge our old beliefs, and we have to risk failure. What do most people do when they need money? Some borrow, and get deeper in debt. Others tighten their belts and adapt their needs to their meager income. Instead of challenging themselves and their world to fulfill their dreams, most people limit their dreams to their perceptions of the world's constraints. They have a passive, wait-and-see attitude -- "Let's see if this miracle happens." And, most often, it doesn't happen. OUR LIVES REFLECT OUR BELIEFS -- UNLIMITED SUCCESS COMES FROM AN UNLIMITED BELIEF SYSTEM To improve your financial situation, to track down a job, to get a raise in your salary, to double your income, to become fit and healthy, you have to passionately want to improve your life. You have to take action, adopt precise measures, and change your attitude. This has to become a fixed objective. This overriding desire is mandatory to create the life you want. Determination and will are all the strength you need. Kazuo Inamori, CEO of Kyocera International and author of A Passion for Success , puts it this way: An entrepreneur must first have a clear vision of what he or she wants. A mere dream of what you want is not adequate. Instead, cultivate a desire so strong and a vision so clear that they become part of your subconscious mind. So many people honestly desire to improve their lives but still fail in their attempts to become successful. The reason is that they have mistaken wishing for wanting . Wishful thinking is far more common than really wanting something. A wish is weak, changeable, and passive. It's not strong enough to overcome procrastination or other obstacles that may arise in the process of getting what you want. Really wanting something is a spur to action. It does not tolerate delays. It bypasses obstacles. It gives us wings to fly. One day a wise man was asked by a disciple what it took to obtain wisdom. The sage led the disciple to a river and plunged his head underwater. After a few seconds, his anxious follower began struggling, afraid he was going to drown. But the teacher continued to hold his head underwater. The student struggled even harder. Finally, the wise man let him go just before he would have drowned and asked him, "When your head was underwater, what did you want most?" "To breathe," the frightened boy answered. "Well, there you have it. That's exactly how much you must want wisdom." And for those of us seeking to improve our lives, that's how much we must want success. Life gives you what you sincerely want. James Allen wrote in his classic work As You Think , "If you cherish a vision, a lofty ideal in your heart, you will realize it....You will become as great as your dominant aspiration." If you content yourself with mediocrity, that is what you will have. Since you're reading this book, you're probably not completely satisfied with your situation. But this dissatisfaction is a gift, as there is something intensely motivating about dissatisfaction: it fuels dreams. As we mentioned before, many successful people had difficult, impoverished childhoods. They felt humiliated. Their desire to rise above poverty and low social status was so intense that it propelled them toward their dreams. It is important to bear in mind, however, that even if you have high aspirations, you will still encounter obstacles. "Even with such strong desires, circumstances will change . . ." Inamori says. "Still, do not use these circumstances as excuses. Your determination should be so strong as to overcome any obstacles, foreseen or unforeseen." The dreams you carry and nourish in your heart are your most noble part. Those who stop dreaming, those who ignore their most intense yearnings are living a life of emptiness and frustration. Don't let this happen to you. Change your life by daring to let yourself be carried away by your dreams and to live out your dreams to the fullest. This philosophy may appear naive -- it is .Without naivete, without the innocence of dreams, nothing great would have been created in this world. Humans would not fly; epic films would not have been made; Ford wouldn't have created the mass-produced automobile; Edison wouldn't have lit the world. A serious outlook, cynicism, and even strictly rational thought are great obstacles to success. We aren't arguing in favor of extravagant, irrational behavior. Far from it! The truth is: At the root of every great discovery and exceptional success story lies a dream, an aspiration, a desire. This desire transcends cynicism and strictly rational thought.

Mind is the master power that molds and makes, And we are mind, and evermore we take The tool of thought, and shaping what we will, Bring forth a thousand joys, a thousand ills. We think in secret, and it comes to pass, Our world is but our looking glass. -- JAMES ALLEN, AUTHOR OF AS YOU THINK T he most common mistake we make is looking outside ourselves for what we can only find inside. Success is no exception. Just as the source of true happiness lies within each of us, success also comes from within. Success is the result of a very specific mental attitude. Call it what you like: the mentality of the rich, an attitude of success, prosperity consciousness. Success is the outward manifestation of an inner focus, the result of steering thoughts toward a specific target. Unfortunately, most people are unaware of this. Most of the principles in the following chapters lead to a higher, universal truth: The mind is capable of anything . Genuine wealth is, above all, a state of mind -- a state that has taken form in the lives of the rich and successful. We have to begin by being rich in mind before we can become rich in life, successful in mind before we can be successful in life. Gaining a clear understanding of the subconscious is fundamental. It's all very well to tell people that they must believe in success and fortune and want it passionately. Yet, most people are paralyzed by bad experiences. They appear completely incapable of cultivating what Friedrich Nietzsche called "the will to power." It's not at all easy to demand action and firmness from someone who is uncertain, indecisive, passive, and unmotivated. By discovering the mechanisms and power of the subconscious mind, however, anyone can overcome these obstacles. OUR SUBCONSCIOUS MIND IS LIMITLESS We are the creators of our own happiness or misery. Truly understanding this statement can be our most important motivator. The key to success ultimately lies in the proper use of the subconscious mind. Both the means to make money and the outside circumstances affecting us are so varied and so personal that it would be impossible to propose a single surefire winning formula to create success. No miracle recipe exists -- but there is a common theme through all success stories. This single, simple theme is a positive inner attitude . Analysis and research only go so far. And then our sixth sense, what some people call business sense or intuition, comes into play -- the result of positive mental programming and a well-utilized subconscious mind. The subconscious mind is best represented by the image of the iceberg: The small, visible part is the conscious mind while the submerged and much larger part is the subconscious. The role of the subconscious in our lives is much greater than most of us understand. It's the seat of our habits, complexes, and the limitations of our personalities. No matter what we think, the subconscious -- not outside circumstances -- is responsible for an individual's success or failure . There are many ways we train our subconscious. One of the strongest ways is through our beliefs. Peter Senge, author of The Fifth Discipline , writes: Most of us hold one of two contradictory beliefs that limit our ability to create what we really want. The more common is the belief in our powerlessness -- our inability to bring into being all the things we really care about. The other belief centers on unworthiness -- that we do not deserve to have what we truly want. . . . There are many ways by which the subconscious gets programmed. Cultures program the subconscious. Beliefs program the subconscious. It is well established, for example, that beliefs affect perception: If you believe that people are untrustworthy, you will continually "see" double-dealing and chicanery that others without this belief would not see. The subconscious can be compared to a computer. It blindly and infallibly executes the program fed into it. An appropriate term from the computer industry is GIGO -- Garbage In, Garbage Out. Much of our programming from infancy onward has been negative garbage, coming straight from negative belief systems. In early childhood, our critical sense is still undeveloped, and we naturally accept all suggestions from the outside world. The program's database, so to speak, comes at first from parents and teachers, media and peers. Their words become engraved in our young minds, which are as impressionable as soft clay. A single word can blight someone's life, or at least weigh them down for a long time. This word may have been said without malice, but if it contained fear and negativity, the effects can be disastrous. A pessimistic mother, one day snapping in frustration, may tell a child she considers too impulsive or whimsical, "Quit dreaming -- stop living in the clouds. Who do you think you are?" These remarks are recorded in the child's subconscious and become part of his or her mental programming. The job of the subconscious, which has almost limitless power, is to execute this program, making the child fail over and over again. The most tragic thing of all is that people who have had this type of early conditioning can spend their entire lives unaware that they are the victims of negative mental programming. Words are extremely powerful agents. A declaration of love, a piece of bad news, a word of congratulations all have a major impact on our inner state. And the words don't even have to be true for the mind to accept them . Thomas Peters and Robert Waterman, authors of In Search of Excellence , describe an experiment that illustrates the power of words, even when those words are untrue: The old adage is "nothing succeeds like success." It turns out to have a sound scientific basis. Researchers studying motivation find that the prime factor is simply the selfperception among motivated subjects that they are, in fact, doing well. Whether they are or not by any absolute standard doesn't seem to matter much. In one experiment, adults were given ten puzzles to solve. All ten were exactly the same for all subjects. They worked on them, turned them in, and were given the results at the end. Now, in fact, the results they were given were fictitious. Half of the exam takers were told that they had done well, with seven out of ten correct. The other half were told they had done poorly, with seven out of ten wrong. Then all were given another ten puzzles (the same for each person). The half who had been told that they had done well in the first round really did do better in the second, and the other half really did do worse. Mere association with past personal success apparently leads to more persistence, higher motivation, or something that makes us do better. The result of this experiment is worth some thought. The subjects' subconscious minds were influenced by the falsified results. Perception alone radically improved one group's performance and weakened the other's. A little further on, the same authors advance the following theory as a result of this experiment: "We often argue that the excellent companies are the way they are because they are organized to obtain extraordinary effort from ordinary human beings." What applies to businesses certainly applies equally to individuals. Their secret: a well-guided subconscious mind. In addition to parents, teachers, and friends who clumsily express negativity without realizing the harmful impact they have, there is another very important programming agent as well: the individual. All of us have our own inner monologues that program us constantly. We repeat to ourselves: "Nothing ever works out for me." "I'm always tired." "What am I doing with my life?" "I'm not appreciated enough." "I'm not good enough." "It's so hard to succeed." "I never have enough time." "I've wasted so much time." The list is endless. These negative, pessimistic thoughts that we repeat to ourselves, more or less consciously, influence or reinforce the current program. But they don't have to stay in our consciousness. When we reach adulthood, we can take responsibility for our own belief systems. No programming has to be permanent. Any negative programming can be turned around. How? Through the power of even a single affirmation that effectively counteracts that negative programming. THE POWER OF AFFIRMATIONS, THE POWER OF SELFSUGGESTION How can we acquire a mentality that will produce favorable circumstances and attract success? There are a wide variety of methods available, all based on some form of self-suggestion. These methods have a number of different names -- mental programming, positive thinking, affirmation, self-hypnosis, psycho-cybernetics, the Alpha method. All of these techniques have proven to be effective. Both authors of this book have experienced wonderful results by using a simple formula, or affirmation, developed by a famous French pharmacist, Emile Coué. Coué's discovery was accidental. One day, one of his clients insisted on buying a drug for which he needed a prescription. He had no prescription, but still stubbornly demanded the drug. Coué thought up a trick: He recommended a product that he said was just as effective, but was actually only a sugar pill. The patient came back a few days later, completely cured and absolutely delighted with the results. What was later called the placebo effect had just been discovered. What had happened to this patient? It was essentially the same phenomenon that had occurred in the experiment in In Search of Excellence , except that the magical effect of words, of confidence, and of the subconscious had acted on the physical rather than the intellectual level. This patient was cured by his confidence in the pharmacist and in the medication, as well as by the mental certainty that he was going to get well. It didn't take Coué long to realize the significance of this experiment. If a word could cure an ailment, what could it do to someone's personality? In the next few years he developed an extremely simple formula, one that involved no sugar pills -- simply words. It has been applied throughout the world and has improved the lives of thousands of individuals. The formula is actually a simple self-suggestion. Since Coué couldn't stay at all of his patients' bedsides, or stay in contact with them, the patients could cure themselves using the formula, which consisted of these words: Every day, in every way, I am getting better and better. Coué advised people to repeat this sentence aloud in a monotone voice at least twenty times a day. Countless variations on the formula have been conceived. We can each concoct our own according to our needs and personality. The effects are astounding. This general formula, this simple affirmation, embraces all aspects of our lives and has limitless possibilities. The golden rule of self-suggestion is repetition, so this should be repeated daily -- throughout the day -- to have the best effect. A relaxed state, where the subconscious is most receptive to new information, is the best -- though not essential. It makes the process effective much more quickly, however. You are naturally in a relaxed state after meditation, upon awakening, or at bedtime. Or relaxation can easily be self-induced: To do this, lie down or seat yourself comfortably in an armchair, and close your eyes. Inhale deeply several times. Then relax each separate part of the body, beginning with the feet, ankles, legs, and on up to the head. You must literally flood your subconscious with your new formula. Little by little, a new program will set in, and a new personality will emerge. Negative reinforcement will give way to positive reinforcement, to enthusiasm, energy, boldness, and determination. Don't be put off by the simplicity of this method, as were many of Coué's contemporaries, who refused to believe that such a simple technique could be effective. As the authors of this book, we're living proof this technique is effective! Try it, several times a day for at least a month, and see the results for yourself. Many successful people, when faced with adversity, have subconsciously resorted to this technique or others like it. Whether confronted by problems or on the threshold of a new adventure, they learned to condition or reprogram themselves by repeating the ideas that they would reach success, that no obstacle would hinder their attempts, that their visions would certainly become reality. The cumulative result of all our inner programming is our self-image . Despite our conscious efforts to create a self-image, each of us has only a vague idea of the one we actually project. We have an even more vague idea of the role self-image plays in our lives. It's important to understand this because people are what they believe themselves to be. Everything in our lives, including our wealth, joy, and physical shape, is directly proportional to our self-image, directly influenced by our self-image. Peter Senge adds another important point: Ultimately, what matters most in developing the subconscious... is the genuine caring for the desired outcome, the deep feeling of it being the "right" goal toward which to aspire. The subconscious seems especially receptive to goals in line with our deeper aspiration and values. According to some spiritual disciplines, this is because these deeper aspirations input directly to, or are part of, the subconscious mind. His words are worth pondering. PICTURE YOUR SUCCESS -- IMAGINE IT CLEARLY What do you want? What does your version of success look like? You are unique; you have a unique definition of success, and success can only come through your unique vision. Those who see themselves as nothing but lowly employees, who can't imagine ever being able to scale the corporate ladder, will stay in lowly positions. "There's no way I can double my income in a year!" If this is what we believe, life proves us right. We always establish our goals according to our self-image. It's therefore just as hard for us to fail as to succeed. And it's just as easy for us to succeed as it is to fail. A new self-image produces a new goal, and a new goal results in a new life. In her powerful book Creative Visualization , Shakti Gawain writes, "Creative visualization is the technique of using your imagination to create what you want in your life." All successful people pictured themselves successful before achieving their dreams. No matter how poor they were in the beginning, no matter how little education they had, no matter how few contacts they had, all of them pictured themselves successful. They became convinced they would be successful. Life answered their dreams in accordance with their self-image and the faith they had in their success. Because of this direct correlation between your self image and what life offers you, it's extremely worthwhile to work on your self-image, so that every day in every way, you are getting better and better . This affirmation does wonders for your self-image. You can change your self-image at any time, according to your aspirations. In the beginning, when you start reprogramming yourself and shaping a new self image, you'll inevitably be influenced by your old image. This is completely natural. Change takes place in gradual stages. But you'll eventually develop a new self-image, and it will produce new goals -- and new goals will, inevitably, change your life for the better. Experience has shown that to be fully effective self-suggestions or affirmations should be: (1) brief -- if they are too long, they will not be effective -- and (2) positive , which is absolutely essential. The subconscious works differently from the conscious mind. If you say, "I'm not poor anymore," the word poor might be subconsciously retained because it is the key word. Repeating the statement with the negative word could produce the opposite results of what you want. You have to take a positive, yet gradual, approach. Some authors write that you must formulate your suggestions as if you already have what you desire: "I am now rich." This could be counterproductive in some cases, however, because your conscious mind might see a contradiction here. Mental conflict could arise to compromise the positive results of the suggestion. If you repeat, "I am now rich," or "My job is perfect," at least some part of your mind will naturally sense the inconsistency, especially if you're broke or out of work. In our opinion, it's better to say, "I'm getting more and more successful, day by day," or "I am creating a perfect job." It's important to find the affirmation that feels positive and empowering for you. Affirmations guarantee success . We know this from experience. Even starting with a mechanical and barely convincing repetition of your words has some effect. The more emotion and feeling you put into your suggestion, however, the better the results will be. Don't impose limitations on your affirmations. Your potential is extraordinary. As Ray Kroc, the founder of McDonald's, said, "Think big and you'll become big."

CREATE A POSITIVE VIEW OF MONEY -- MONEY CAN BE A POWERFUL AGENT OF GOOD IN THE WORLD Through our work we create ideas, innovative products, jobs, beautiful works of art, educational tools, and so on, endlessly. And those who truly understand real success give back to their communities and their world through philanthropy and many other forms of financial and visionary support. There are literally millions of wealthy people who are the opposite of the unscrupulous, mean-spirited money-grubber who seeks materialism for its own sake, for greedy acquisition and consumption. It's no coincidence that the richest countries in the world have also reached the highest achievements in culture and science. Money affords us the time and resources to pursue desires beyond basic human needs, to create things that are as important as survival itself. Money is simply a recognition of services rendered. Most people who become wealthy have provided services to many people and have been justly rewarded for them. Walt Disney brightened the lives of millions of children, and adults as well. The list of contributions made by the wealthy is endless, for money is power -- power to do a great deal of good in the world. Henry Ford was once asked what he would do if he lost his entire fortune. Without a moment's hesitation, he said he would think up another fundamental human need and meet it by offering a cheaper and more efficient service than anybody else. He said that he would be a millionaire again within five years. Many people have an aversion to money. This aversion is often hypocritical: People malign the rich but secretly envy them. Once you begin to understand some of the principles in this book and begin providing the kind of services to humanity that will make you substantial amounts of money, your attitude toward the rich will change completely -- because you'll become one of them. And you'll be able to do a lot of good for a lot of people with your wealth. Another prevalent mental block is the fear of going against family background and upbringing -- outdoing one's parents, for example. Not everyone suffers from this, of course; we have already seen that poverty can be a strong catalyst for success. But in many cases, poverty is a form of neurotic behavior -- a mental rut that goes nowhere, the reflection of an impoverished self-image. Mental blocks around the issue of making money come disguised in a great variety of forms that we need to examine as we recognize them in ourselves. It's important to integrate a positive view of money and success into your new self-image. Be vigilant and honest with yourself; identify your mental blocks and release them. Identify your limiting beliefs and change them.

Replace them with more positive, powerful thoughts. Both poverty and riches are the offspring of thought. THERE ARE NO LIMITATIONS TO THE MIND This is a very powerful truth, one that bears repeating: There are no limitations to the mind except those we accept . Once we understand this as a truth, we can become successful and shape our present and future life to match our aspirations. When we apply this truth to our lives, our circumstances become whatever we desire; our lives become whatever we want them to be. If you steer your thoughts in a positive, expansive direction, you'll become as powerful as you can imagine. Every day, make sure that you devote some time to reprogramming yourself, to creative visualization, guided imagery, daydreaming. Many people are paid extraordinary salaries to daydream! Our most lucrative thoughts can come through daydreaming, free-rambling fantasy, and brainstorming future possibilities. Daydreams are often maligned by "down-to-earth" people who say that we have to look life squarely in the face and accept our fate, even if it leaves a lot to be desired. Yet, these resigned and unhappy individuals forget that there are two types of dreamers: those who make no attempt to turn their dreams into reality, and those who understand and believe in the creative power of the subconscious. These are the dreamers who take concrete measures to fulfill their dreams. These are the dreamers who shape our world and who create wealth for themselves and others in the process. In The Seven Spiritual Laws of Success , Deepak Chopra says: Inherent in every intention and desire is the mechanics for its fulfillment. Intention and desire in the field of pure potentiality have infinite organizing power. And when we introduce an intention in the fertile ground of pure potentiality, we put this infinite organizing power to work for us. Let's examine what Chopra is saying. If intention is thought and our thoughts are filled with negative ideas toward money (we can only make enough to get by, for example, or there is never enough), we will fulfill these thoughts. If, however, we fill our mind with new and positive images (there are no limits, as the universe contains infinite possibilities), we will fulfill these thoughts, and become as successful as we can possibly imagine. Clearly imagine that you already have what you hope for, that you have reached your goals. What does your life look like? One reason this exercise of imagination is so effective is that the subconscious is not governed by the same rules of time as the conscious mind. In fact, time doesn't exist in the subconscious mind -- or in our dreams, which are the subconscious mind's most easily recognizable by-product. This is why trauma experienced in early childhood can affect people long after they are adults; rational minds understand that they no longer have to worry about the past, but the subconscious may not recognize the difference. This is also why we can pretend that something is true in our fantasies and our visualizations, and the subconscious mind will go about its work and bring what we imagine into reality, whether the things we imagine are our fears or our ardent desires for the very best. This may seem to contradict what we said earlier (on page 40) about affirmations. In our fantasies and visualizations, however, it is very effective to imagine as fully as possible that we have created the future we dream of. OUR THOUGHTS MATERIALIZE All of our thoughts tend to materialize in our lives when they are repeated enough. This is why, in order to succeed, we have to monitor our thoughts closely. If we continually focus on financial troubles, we invite them to stay. Wherever you focus your attention, wherever you put your energy, that is what will grow. If you focus on the good that you want, you welcome abundance, prosperity, and success. If you focus on how little money you bring home every month, you will continue to experience frustration and need. However, if you focus on putting even a small amount away -- just ten dollars a week in a savings account, for example -- and imagine the account growing, you will begin to create abundance in your life because your focus will shift from "lack of " to "growth." Try it, and you'll be amazed at how different it feels to focus on growth rather than lack, on prosperity rather than poverty. The subconscious is a vast field, governed by the universal law of cause and effect. As we sow, so we reap. Thoughts and ideas are the cause; facts and events are the effect. Most people have more imagination for conjuring up problems that prevent them from realizing their dreams than for recognizing their opportunities for success. Stephen Covey, author of The Seven Habits of Highly Effective People , emphasizes this point: Habits have tremendous gravity pull. Like any natural force, gravity pull can work with us or against us. The gravity pull of some of our habits may currently be keeping us from going where we want to go. Breaking deeply imbedded habitual tendencies such as procrastination, impatience, criticalness, or selfishness that violate basic principles of human effectiveness involves more than a little willpower and a few minor changes in our lives. It takes tremendous effort to break free from the gravity pull of such habits, but once we do, our freedom takes on a whole new dimension. Change -- real change -- comes from the inside out....It comes from striking at the root -- the fabric of our thought, the fundamental, essential paradigms, which give definition to our character and create the lens through which we see the world. Successful people are inspired by their dreams, and they focus on the means to reach them, not on what's keeping them from realizing them. Inventors see their inventions. Artists see their completed works. Successful entrepreneurs see their businesses thriving. Visionaries, social workers, nonprofit workers, and even some politicians see society changed for the better. Ted Turner, creator of a broadcast empire, said, "A visionary is supposed to have a vision of the future." Ideas govern the world. The power they have is phenomenal. It is therefore necessary to repeatedly fill our minds with thoughts of service, abundance, and success -- to break free of the gravity pull of our negative thoughts. Eventually, we replace the old, negative thoughts with a new, positive self-image. Each thought has energy and, through some mysterious law of attraction, draws objects, beings, and circumstances of a similar nature to it -- like a magnet. Negative thoughts attract negative experiences. Positive thoughts attract positive experiences. Unfortunately, this truth is not always supported by society. Our educational system generally supports and encourages the rational and strictly logical part of thought, while neglecting or even scorning its intuitive and imaginative side. The right side of the brain is too often ignored. And yet nothing great has ever been achieved without an original dream. A dream is a kind of projection of our inner selves. What, in fact, is a projection or a project? By definition, it's something that we throw forward. We project even our own self-images, and this projection in turn programs our minds to create success or failure depending on the quality of the projection. The greater we program our self-images to be, the more expansive our dreams will be. And our dreams, however bold, are often more easily attainable than we might even believe at the time that we form them. Steven Spielberg once dreamed of making a certain film. He had the script, but he needed a producer to finance it. One day, while walking on the beach, he "accidentally" met a rich man who was ready to invest in young filmmakers. With the money Spielberg received from this producer, a total stranger to him at the time, he was able to shoot Amblin , which was given an Honorable Mention at the Venice Film Festival and drew attention to him in Hollywood. This is often how the subconscious solves a problem: We have a chance encounter, or we happen to see an article or TV show that provides a clear-cut answer to a dilemma, or our family or friends somehow contribute to our success -- sometimes in ways they aren't even aware of at the time. When others point to fate, or to difficult circumstances, believing we need to be "resigned to our fate," we point out that the world is governed mentally and physically by cause and effect, and so we create our fate; it's the result of our thoughts and actions. The same is true for good and bad luck: They're the consequences of our thoughts and actions. We literally make our own good and bad luck. This is why people who correctly learn and apply the laws of the mind and success forge their own destiny. The supreme secret of success is a secret not because anyone is trying to keep it secret but only because so few understand it. This secret can be told in a few simple words, and success will come to you when you truly understand these words: The human mind can accomplish whatever it believes in. Henry Ford summed it up very well in his now-famous quote: "Whether you think you can or you think you can't, you're right."

Preface

"When rich people get together they don't talk about saving money; they talk about the other side of the ledger, how to make money with money. They talk about all sorts of businesses they are into to augment their paycheck and create even more wealth. "Yet, the vast majority of financial self-help books are all about trying to make ends meet, about trying to take a little bit of money and conserve it. Some might focus on how to invest better in the stock market. But almost none talk about what the wealthy talk about when they chat: making big money on the money they have. "Arvind's book may be the first I have read that doesn't patronize you or try to keep you from making the big money I know you have the ability to make with some help, help from Arvind.

_____ indian readers

There has never been more personal wealth in India than there is today . Yet most Indian are not wealthy. Nearly one-half of our wealth is owned by 3.5 percent of our households. Most of the other households don't even come close. By "other households," we are not referring to economic dropouts. Most of these millions of households are composed of people who earn moderate, even high, incomes. More than twenty-five million households in the INDIA have annual incomes in excess of 6,00000Rs more than seven million have annual incomes over 12,0000. But in spite of being "good income" earners, too many of these people have small levels of accumulated wealth. Many live from paycheck to paycheck. These are the people who will benefit most from this book.

Only a minority of Indian have even the most conventional types of financial assets. Only about 15 percent of Indian households have a money market deposit account; 22 percent, a certificate of deposit; 4.2 percent, a money market fund; 3.4 percent, corporate or municipal bonds; fewer than 25 percent, stocks and mutual funds; 8.4 percent, rental property; 18.1 percent, U.S. Savings Bonds; and 23 percent, IRA or KEOGH accounts.

But 65 percent of the households have equity in their own home, and more than 85 percent own one or more motor vehicles. Cars tend to depreciate rapidly. Financial assets tend to appreciate. The millionaires we discuss in this book are financially independent. They could maintain their current lifestyle for years and years without earning even one month's pay. The large majority of these millionaires are not the descendants of the Rockefellers or Vanderbilts. More than 80 percent are ordinary people who have accumulated their wealth in one generation. They did it slowly, steadily, without signing a multimillion-dollar contract with the Yankees, without winning the lottery, without becoming the next Mick Jagger. Windfalls make great headlines, but such occurrences are rare. In the course of an adult's lifetime, the probability of becoming wealthy via such paths is lower than one in four thousand. Contrast these odds with the proportion of American households (3.5 per one hundred) in the $1 million and over net worth category.

Prologue

DO WHAT YOU LOVE I believe if you have talent and skill, you should spin off on your own and become captain of your own destiny. -- GEORGE LUCAS, FILMMAKER AND FOUNDER AND CHAIRMAN OF LUCAS ARTS I would love to set up my own business, but I don't have the ability or financing." "My dream was to become an actor, but my parents laughed at the idea. I work for the government instead." "My job bores me to tears, but there's so much unemployment and downsizing going on that I'd better not kid myself about finding a better one." "I used to dream of being a lawyer, but it would take years." How often have we heard words like these, or variations on the same themes? How often have you had similar thoughts? Out of every ten people, how many can boast of really enjoying their jobs? Unfortunately, most people simply don't like what they do for a living. They're convinced that they're stuck in their drudgery, that they will never be able to change their situations. Fate, in other words, has permanently sentenced them to a life of mediocrity. If you dislike your job, consider the following: You could die without having done what you really want to do. Aren't you worth more than that? Take a typical day in the life of so many people: They work eight hours at a job they don't particularly enjoy, and then sleep eight hours. This leaves them with eight hours they typically use to recover and to try to forget the frustrations heaped on them during the day. Their dissatisfaction affects their relationships with their spouses, children, and friends. And yet, they continue, believing they must . Most people unwillingly drag themselves to work on Monday morning and watch the clock until Friday afternoon, when they can finally throw off the shackles they had to endure for five long, painful days. They only really live for two out of seven days, with Saturday generally spent winding down or getting life's necessities together, and Sunday already haunted by the gloomy specter of Monday-morning blues. And they tolerate this, year after year. This passive, fatalistic view of life can be changed. Nothing obliges you to keep working at a job you don't like. You can do something about it. An inspiring job exists to fulfill everyone's passion. And you could start it right now. Is life so poorly designed that it's meant to frustrate us constantly and deprive us of what we truly want? Life isn't that cruel. At least, it doesn't have to be. It's your choice . LIFE GIVES US EXACTLY WHAT WE EXPECT The belief that dreams are impossible to achieve prevents most people from getting what they want. Their experience certainly seems to support this belief. They get exactly what they expect from life: boredom, frustration, obstacles, and small incomes. People are what they believe themselves to be, no more, no less. Denying your personal inclinations and ambitions normally begins very early in life. Yet, to be happy and fulfilled, we have to be courageous enough to be ourselves, to discover what we want, and to go after it. We have to stop denying ourselves because of fear, doubt, or conformity to some "normal" behavior or way of life. It's a fallacy that we have to do unfulfilling things to earn a living. In fact, to be successful, you have to first do what you enjoy in life. If you don't enjoy your work, you can't do it well. This is an absolute principle. When your heart isn't in something, you experience a drastic slump in energy and motivation. You inevitably come up with mediocre results, or at least with a much poorer performance than you would if you loved what you were doing. It then follows that your boss, associates, clients, or customers can't be completely satisfied with what you have accomplished. As an unhappy employee, chances are slim that you will get promoted to a more interesting position or receive a substantial raise. As an unhappy business owner, chances are small that your business will flourish. Since you rarely work alone, your unhappiness can drag your colleagues down. The monetary rewards you get will reflect this. And with poor monetary compensation, your motivation and the quality of your work plummets -- another vicious cycle! Mark McCormack, author of What They Don't Teach You at Harvard Business School , makes this excellent point: Boredom occurs when the learning curve flattens out. It can happen to anyone at any level of the corporation. In fact, it occurs most often in successful people who need more challenge and stimulation than do others. If you're bored it's your fault. You just aren't working hard enough at making your job interesting. It is also probably the reason you haven't been offered anything better. Find out what you love to do and you will be successful at it. DO WHAT YOU LOVE When we say -- emphatically -- that you must love your work, we are in no way suggesting that an ideal job will be devoid of frustration, disappointment, and problems. Every successful person has faced periods of discouragement, frustration, and even self-doubt. Your dream job will not be heaven on earth every day. It's more like true love: The deep bonds that bring and keep two people together allow them to overcome the dilemmas and obstacles that appear along the way. Thomas Watson, founder of IBM, said it this way: "Make room in your heart for work and put some heart into your work." Successful people are ruled by passion and their hearts. They are romantics, whether in art or in the world of business. They are spurred into action by their love of their work and their desire to do new things, to take up new challenges, to face new risks. They carry their dreams in their hearts -- and they do everything they can to achieve them. PASSION AND POWER In Work with Passion , author Nancy Anderson defines passion: Passion is intense emotional excitement. It is a feeling that comes to those who feel intensely about some object, person, ideal, or belief. Human passions are released to create both good and evil. There are many examples in history that show the difference one passionate person can make. Every love story, every major change in history -- social, economic, philosophical, and artistic -- came about because of the participation of passionate individuals. We all have the capacity to feel intense emotional excitement. However, few of us act on our passions. We bury our passion because, among other reasons, we were ridiculed early in life because our enthusiasm was not backed up with expertise. As soon as you give yourself permission to feel whatever you feel, that power will resurface, surprising all who "knew you when." Then you will take action on those feelings. Power is the ability to take action . As an adult, you know that your decisions are your choices. It is no longer necessary to do anything you hate -- you can choose to do only what you truly love to do. That is power. That is passion in action. Here's a good question to ask yourself: If you won ten million dollars, would you stay in your present job? If your answer is "yes," congratulations! If not, then creating a situation in which you would answer "yes" to that question could be a very important goal. Here are a few principles to move you toward this goal: * The only way to be happy and successful is to do what you truly enjoy doing. There is an ideal job or career for each one of us, a service that we can provide that no one else can do in quite the same way. * You can do whatever you like, provided you put the necessary energy and determination into it. * You alone can shape your destiny and decide to do what you enjoy, regardless of obstacles. The greatest barrier to success is yourself. * Dare to do what you love. Overcome your fear-based mental and emotional blocks and you will succeed. William O'Brian of Hanover Insurance puts it this way in an interview with Peter Senge in The Fifth Discipline : "To seek personal fulfillment only outside of work and to ignore the significant portion of our lives that we spend working would be to limit our opportunities to be happy and complete human beings." BECOME THE BEST AT WHAT YOU

DO In his autobiography, Henry Ford said, "I determined absolutely that never would I join a company in which finance came before the work." For Ford, "the only foundation of real business is service." Success is built on service. Successful service is built on one attitude: the attitude of doing the best we can, working to be the best in our field. Many successful people are motivated into action by the need to do things well and to accomplish something that will help other people. Making a profit is not their primary purpose, yet they usually make far more money than those who work primarily for profit. Steve Jobs, founder of Apple Computer, has said, "We're doing this because we really care about the higher educational process, not because we want to make a buck." Wealth is the reward we receive in exchange for services we render. If we give the best service, then we can expect a commensurate reward. It is very powerful, then, to program our subconscious toward becoming the best in our field in a given period of time. As we give ourselves completely to our gift -- our service -- our gift gives back to us abundantly. BECOME AN EXPERT IN YOUR CHOSEN FIELD While you don't necessarily have to pursue years of formal education, it's invaluable to pursue all avenues to becoming an expert in your field. In the world today, when last month's computer system is already out of date, you have to keep up with change. One of the fundamentals of success is having in-depth knowledge or specialization in your work. A lack of knowledge is one of the major roadblocks to success. Start by considering the products or services you have to offer to the public before looking for profits. With a good product or service, money comes naturally. When you become the best in your field, and focus on serving, the money will follow. This is an ancient law that never fails. BE AN ORIGINAL Formal education is certainly not sufficient to guarantee success. Something more is needed -- a spark of originality or boldness, which schools often fail to teach and sometimes stifle altogether. All too often, schools level out the thinking process and suppress the creativity that allows you to see new possibilities and original solutions. Education, and society in general, too often nip personal aspirations in the bud. This insidious process begins early in life. Our fears of being different and our need to conform support the part of our subconscious programming that limits our dreams, ideas, and aspirations. We all naturally imitate those around us, especially when we 're young. Unfortunately, the vast majority of people have imitated passionless jobs, financial struggle, and mediocrity. A small, inner voice nevertheless survives within each of us. Timid and worried, it whispers to us that our public images are false, that our genuine personalities are hidden and unexpressed. Frustration, sadness, and, in some cases, a dead feeling inside are some of the burdens we heap upon ourselves when we deny who we are and what we have to offer. If we want to succeed, we have to be different. We have to fully be ourselves and not be afraid to assert our true personalities. We are unique individuals with a unique purpose in life. Each of us is an original. MAKE YOUR DESIRES INTO INTENTIONS, AND MAKE THEM CRYSTAL CLEAR "I don't have the faintest idea what I really want to do. . . ." Sound familiar? This is an all-toocommon complaint. So many people are overwhelmed with confusion, and yet they never sit down and ask themselves the simplest questions -- the kind of questions we ask throughout this book. The answers to these questions would dissolve their confusion in an instant. When people complain about not knowing what they want to do with their lives, it's obvious they have spent years stifling their aspirations and ignoring their inner selves. By conforming to other people 's expectations and ways of life, they have forgotten who they are and have sowed the seeds of their confusion. Anyone who doesn't really know what he or she wants to do and doesn't establish clear-cut goals will find it hard to succeed. The opposite is also true: When we know perfectly well what we want to do in life, when our desire is crystal clear, the conditions enabling us to achieve it soon appear. Often, extremely precise desires are fulfilled almost immediately. A perfectly straightforward desire -- devoid of hesitation, ambiguity, and contradiction -- is very rare indeed. Vague, confused ambitions create a muddled subconscious. Since our aspirations are unclear, the results will be nebulous. A metamorphosis has to take place within -- we have to form a clear picture of our ambitions and desires. We have to sculpt them to be clear and precise. Don't underestimate the importance of this inner change. Until we are sure what we want, we won't get it. All successful people have unmistakable, clear ambitions and intentions. Their career choices were spawned by a deep sense of intuition that left no room for doubt. One of the most powerful keys to success, therefore, is knowing exactly what you want to be, do, and have. Deepak Chopra's words are worth repeating here: "Inherent in every intention and desire is the mechanics for its fulfillment." In The Seven Spiritual Laws of Success , Chopra illuminates intention and desire in more detail, and adds another very important element of true, lasting success: detachment . Intention lays the groundwork for the effortless, spontaneous, frictionless flow of pure potentiality seeking expression from the unmanifest to the manifest.... Intention is the real power behind desire. Intent alone is very powerful, because intent is desire without attachment to the outcome. Desire alone is weak, because desire in most people is intention with attachment....Intention combined with detachment leads to life centered, present-moment awareness. And when action is performed in presentmoment awareness, it is most effective. Your intent is for the future, but your attention is in the present. As long as your attention is in the present, then your intent for the future will manifest, because the future is created in the present. Accept the present and intend the future. The future is something you can always create through detached intention. Turn your wishes into crystal-clear desires . Turn your desires into intentions . Once you intend to do something, 90 percent of your perceived obstacles vanish -- and you have the tools to overcome the remaining 10 percent. Such is the power of your intent! When you make an absolutely clear intention to do something, and yet are not attached to the results, you have an infallible formula for success and fulfillment. SUMMARY AND RECOMMENDED ACTION To integrate passion and power in your work life and to become the best at what you do: 1. Think about your life as it is; then picture how you want it to be. If you're not doing what you like, make a list of all of the reasons you can think of that support your belief that you can't do what truly excites and pleases you. Now go over the list point by point and think about each reason. Are these obstacles really valid? If you can understand the principles in this book, you will understand that every obstacle can be overcome and turned into an opportunity. As Henry Ford said, "Whether you think you can or you think you can't, you're right." 2. Ask yourself, if you had all the time and money in the world, what would you do? If you would still do what you currently do, then you are on the right track, because you are passionate about what you do. If you would rather be doing something else, ask yourself: In what ways can I do the things I want now? How can I begin to live the life I want to live ideally? 3. Become aware of your inner dialogue, as often as you possibly can. Life gives you exactly what you expect. You write your own script in the drama of life, with every word you think and say -- so it's up to you to write a better script for yourself. 4. In a relaxed state, repeat the following affirmations, or formulas for success, to yourself: * I am unique. I have something to offer. * It is my right and duty to be myself. * I am becoming successful. I invite success and prosperity into my life. * I attract the people and situations that will help me offer my service. * Every day, in every way, I am getting better and better. 5. At night, ask your subconscious to help you discover how you can be a complete success, make all the money you want, and serve humanity and the earth. Fall asleep knowing that the answer already lies within you, and that you have already obtained what you asked for. The formidable power of your subconscious will work continuously, night and day, as long as you have steered it in the right direction. I resolved first to make enough money so I'd never be stopped from finishing anything. -- WILLIAM P. LEAR, LEAR JET INC. O nce we have discovered our passion, the field in which we want to succeed, we can concentrate on fulfilling our plans. Some of the best plans are the simplest. Thomas Peters and Robert Waterman's In Search of Excellence discusses the paradox of simplicity: Many of today's managers -- MBA-trained and the like -- may be a little bit too smart for their own good. The smart ones are the ones who shift direction all the time, based upon the latest output from the expected value equation. The ones who juggle hundredvariable models with facility; the ones who design complicated incentive systems; the ones who wire up matrix structures; the ones who have 200-page strategic plans and 500-page market requirement documents that are but step one in product development exercises. Our "dumber" friends are different. They just don't understand why every customer can't have personalized service, even in the potato chip business. They are personally affronted ...when a bottle of beer goes sour. They can't understand why a regular flow of new products isn't possible, or why a worker can't contribute a suggestion every couple of weeks. Simpleminded fellows, really; simplistic even. Yes, simplistic has a negative connotation. But the people who lead the excellent companies are a bit simplistic. To believe that we can make as much money as we want, to believe in our dreams, to disregard negative people, we need a good dose of naivete and simplicity. People who are too rational or intelligent can succeed, but their intelligence can limit the degree of their success if it limits in any way the vast field of their dreams. MAKE ONE CLEAR GOAL People who don't succeed don't have precise goals. Any objectives they do have are, on some deep level, invariably low. They succeed at mediocrity or failure. Some people don't even begin to set goals because of the overwhelmingly negative conversations they carry on in their subconscious. Almost all successful people started achieving their dreams only when they set clear goals and timelines for meeting them. (There may be some people who are exceptions to this rule -- but we don't know of any.) Set a precise goal, with a precise amount of income, and a time plan to make it. You'll discover that this is an important difference between those who succeed and those who don't. We achieve what we plan to achieve, no more, no less. There is a story often repeated in business books about the salesman who could never sell more than $25,000 worth of his product in a month. He was assigned to a territory where average sales were well below that amount, and he managed to sell $25,000 a month -- quite an achievement for that territory. His manager sent him to a larger area where other salespeople were performing much better than that. His result: $25,000 a month. The dilemma he faced was clearly based on his goals and self-image. He didn't believe he could sell more (or less) than $25,000 a month, and his subconscious was set accordingly. This story is a good example of the power of the subconscious and the fact that we achieve any objective our subconscious sets for us. Haven't your own experiences been directly linked to your objectives? Anyone with a vague, uncertain target -- or no target at all -- will get vague results, or no results at all. On the other hand, anyone who establishes a specific goal, backed with a specific plan of action, achieves it. Why is this? The answer is within our subconscious mind: A clear target is the most simple and effective way of programming your subconscious. You won't necessarily have to work harder to achieve this goal; you might even have to work less. In the past, success has often been equated with long hours of hard work. But you'll soon find that when you align yourself with your purpose, release negativity, and program yourself for reaching your goals, you achieve results with less effort. It is possible to work less and get better results. A great many people know this is true. The secret lies in making a clear goal. Even among the hardworking and success-oriented, a great many people don't have a specific objective in mind. Many people are satisfied with a slight improvement in their lives without ever considering or daring to set themselves a clear-cut figure that represents a substantial improvement in their lives, something that moves them toward the kind of life they ideally want to live. What is your goal for next year? How much do you want to earn? $50,000? $100,000? $500,000? A million dollars? If you want your lifestyle to improve substantially -- a perfectly legitimate desire -- ask yourself what goal you have to set. If you want a brighter future, establish your goals and determine how much time and energy you are willing and able to channel into reaching them. If all you can do is dream of getting a promotion or a fantastic job offer, but you don't have a specific objective, the "miracle" you are expecting will not happen. Your self-worth is exactly what you think it is. Every successful person realizes this is an obvious truth: If you make a clear goal and begin to take the next apparent steps toward its realization -- whatever steps are required to convince your subconscious you are serious about focusing on that goal -- you will soon find you have reached it. YOU ARE WORTH MUCH MORE THAN YOU BELIEVE The greatest limitations people impose on themselves are created in their own minds. A person's worth is exactly what he or she believes it to be, no more, no less. Most people underestimate themselves, even if they appear self-confident. Those who know, deep down, that they are truly valuable are few and far between. Almost everyone has some degree of an inferiority complex, and this causes them to believe they are unworthy of success, of other people 's esteem, or of much money. The best way to increase your worth is to build your self-esteem. We have already presented techniques useful for bringing about fundamental change. One of the best ways of accomplishing this is to work with a specific monetary objective. SETTING YOURSELF AN EXACT OBJECTIVE IS TRULY MAGICAL Usually the first time you set yourself a specific monetary goal, you retain a certain amount of skepticism that limits the clarity and power of your ambition. So, make your first goals realistic; then, when you achieve your first goal, you can set yourself an even higher goal. Make this goal more of a stretch . Those who set themselves a clear target for the first time are generally surprised when they reach it and often go beyond it! Challenge yourself to reach your goal. It's an exciting game that brings rewarding dividends. Perhaps you'll reach your goal in six months instead of the year you initially gave yourself. We've seen this happen many times. Setting yourself an exact objective is truly magical. YOU ARE WORTH INFINITELY MORE THAN YOU BELIEVE It's not an exaggeration -- it's the truth: You are worth infinitely more than you believe. The only problem is, quite possibly, no one has ever told you that before. Some people have probably tried their best to persuade you that the opposite is true. Intelligence, work, motivation, imagination, discipline, and experience are, of course, important ingredients for success -- but how many people do you know who have these qualities but still don't succeed, or don't live up to their full potential? Perhaps the same is true for you. Despite your obvious talents and efforts, success inexplicably escapes you. You meet people at work or at other companies who don't appear to be any more specially gifted than you, but yet they get the raise, the promotion, and achieve an enviable level of success. Keep this in mind: Their self-images have determined their goals, which have determined their lifestyles. And your self-image has determined your goals, which have determined your lifestyle. Overcome your mental limitations and increase your self-worth by aiming as high as possible. It's not any harder for your subconscious to help you reach a higher objective than a lower one. And it's certainly much more enjoyable! Make your goal a magnificent obsession. Write it down in several places to keep it well in sight. Above all, keep it constantly in mind. A major principle ruling the mind is that energy goes wherever your thoughts go . By repeatedly thinking of your goal and making it a fixed idea, all your energy channels itself into helping you be successful. And thanks to the continuous work of your subconscious, circumstances and people will help you reach your goal in new and surprising ways. MAKE YOUR GOAL A SINGLE, FIXED IDEA A goal is like a magnifying glass: As a magnifying glass can focus the sun's energy to ignite a fire, a goal focuses your energy to make your objective a reality. Make your primary goal into a single, simple, fixed idea. This fixed idea not only allows you to increase your energy and level of success but also prevents a very serious mistake -- scattering your energy. A fixed goal inevitably leads you to success. The single-mindedness of a fixed idea also enables you to direct your professional and personal life more clearly, and with less effort. Everything that brings you closer to your goal should be encouraged. And you should let go of everything that distances you from it. How can you tell if something is bringing you closer or not? Your intuition will tell you in its usual way: a subtle feeling, a comment from a friend or partner, a phrase in a book or an article that resonates with truth for you.

Arvind is the author of more then 50 books you can buy read other book by arvind upadhyay.

arvind upadhyay books

Arvind Upadhyay

Author

Overview   Books

How to Start a Company:...
2021

Essays That Will Change...
2021

Believe in Yourself Yo...
2021

Story of Top

How to Be

Search on google Arvnd upadhayay book

CHAPTER ONE

A PLAN OF ACTION

I believe the decision to focus your efforts is extremely important, not only in the early days of a company but later on as well. -- DAVID PACKARD, HEWLETT-PACKARD T he most vital step on your path to success is preparing a step-by-step plan of action so that your intention becomes solidified, consciously and subconsciously. What actually unfolds may be quite different from your step-by-step plan -- in fact, it probably will be quite different -- but you'll reach the goal, nonetheless, soon after your intention is solid and unwavering. Some jobs, unfortunately, will never bring great financial rewards; if money simply doesn't matter to you, so much the better. But if you want financial security and the means to pursue your dreams, change jobs, if necessary. Look for a position in a field that is compatible with your passion, talents, and skills, and offers a good salary as well. Or start your own business -- in your spare time, if necessary. No human being is infallible, not even the most experienced businessperson. Only those who do nothing never make mistakes. Even if you undergo temporary setbacks, you will still achieve your goals, provided your subconscious is properly programmed. This is the power of a precise monetary goal and a plan of action with a deadline. PREPARE A STEP-BY-STEP PLAN OF ACTION TO SOLIDIFY YOUR INTENTIONS A step-by-step plan of action convinces your subconscious that your desire, your dream, your wishful thinking has become an intention . You intend to accomplish this goal and create this situation in your life. The proof of your intention is your step-by-step plan. Convinced, your unlimited subconscious goes to work. You create exactly what you intend to create -- no more, no less. Applying your plan of action can mean taking risks that cause significant personal insecurity, especially if it's the first time you have set a goal and established a clear plan of action. Almost any change -- even a change for the better -- generates a certain amount of anxiety. Most people's need for security is so great that they are prepared to sacrifice their most precious dreams for it. Don't be afraid to forge ahead. You'll never regret it. We don't know of anyone who ever regretted taking a risk, when it was a step toward realizing a dream. We recommend that you not set more than two separate goals in one area of your life at a time. Pursuing too many goals at once diffuses your concentration and makes your work less effective. Pursuing goals in different areas of your life simultaneously, however, such as career, home, fitness, improved relationships, or finishing the next draft of your thesis or book is advantageous; each improvement benefits the other areas of your life. Another highly beneficial action is to set goals for your future: one year, five years, ten, twenty-five, even fifty years into the future. Where do you want to be when you are sixty? What kind of person would you like to be when you are eighty? What kind of life are you dreaming of? How about your health and fitness? Do you want to have children? What do you want to have accomplished? Don't limit yourself . Sit down and prepare a step-bystep plan. We know many people who have written out a step-by-step plan for something, put it away somewhere and forgotten about it, and then discovered later they had fulfilled their plan, without even consciously thinking about it! We don't recommend this, of course -- we recommend a healthy amount of repetition of your goals -- but we have seen it happen many times. YOU ARE THE ARCHITECT OF YOUR LIFE -- HOW WOULD YOU LIKE TO CREATE IT? Disregard your present situation, your previous failures, your past. Forget about your age, as well. Many people well into their sixties and seventies know the best is yet to come. We can make our lives rich and full at any age. Often the dreams we nourish come true more easily than we expect -- regardless of our age or current situation. When you can picture yourself in an ideal future, when you know what you would like to do for the rest of your life, your short-term goals become far more clear and meaningful. You have a reason to get out of bed every morning and take steps that bring you closer to fulfillment. You have charted the course of your life. You have become a visionary. Picturing your life in this way -- imagining your ideal scene -- can literally shape your future, because through positive dreaming, through creative visualization, you program your subconscious. You flood it with images that are likely to come true. You hold the reins of command. You are indeed the architect of your life. Your blueprints are your goals and your ideal scene of your life in the future. Your long-term goals not only define your ideal in life, they help to create it. They simplify many choices that would otherwise seem difficult or, worse still, arbitrary or absurd. When you don't know what you want to do with your life, it's difficult sometimes to make even the most insignificant dayto-day decisions. They don't seem part of a greater plan that gives meaning to your thoughts and actions. Making a life plan is stimulating and motivating, and it contributes to success in all areas of life. Keep in mind, however, the need to remain flexible regarding the future, since life involves constant adaptation. What you are doing in five or ten years may not necessarily be what you expect -- it might be much better than you ever dreamed possible. When our minds are well programmed, the situations that develop are always better than our previous situations. Every day, in every way, we get better and better. As we develop, our full potential becomes more and more realized, and the plans we dream up are bolder, more ambitious, more expansive. We often drop some of our initial plans along the way, usually because we were "thinking too small." As our self-image expands, our success in the world expands as well. We end up constantly progressing toward greater self-fulfillment -- and personal enrichment, if that's one of our goals. Now carefully plan your main objective for the next year -- while still remaining flexible enough to respond to unforeseen opportunities that may very well come up. You'll have a clear picture of the work and effort you must put in to reach your goal. Divide your yearly goal into months, and then into weeks. Sound planning prevents a lot of worry and delay, and it keeps you moving forward toward your goal. CHARACTER EQUALS DESTINY It is all well and good to set an objective -- it is necessary for anyone wishing to be successful -- but to try to work toward it day by day requires discipline. And the best discipline is the one we, and no one else, impose on ourselves. The Greek philosopher Heraclitus said, "Character equals destiny." If we look around at all the people we know, we see there are no exceptions to this rule. All successful women and men have strong character and are highly disciplined, each in their own way. No one succeeds without strength of character. To become our own master and take our destiny in hand, we need discipline. By discipline, we don't mean a rigid schedule that excludes fantasy and relaxation. And we certainly don't mean workaholism. Discipline also means allowing enough time to rest, exercise, and properly nourish our bodies, enough time to meet family commitments, enough time for fun, enough time to be alone. Overwork is never productive. Complaining of overwork is fashionable these days -- and since most people don't use a tenth of their potential, they are overworked but never seem to accomplish much. They work too hard, and still lack discipline. They haven't created the habits that lead to success. SUCCESS IS A HABIT Discipline and positive mental programming lead naturally to developing our own methods and ways of organization, discovering our personal working rhythm and patterns, and creating the habit of success. Until now, failure or mediocrity has simply been a habit. By replacing one habit with another, our new habit becomes second nature. Success is then irresistibly attracted to us. As the old saying goes: "Sow a thought, and you reap an action; sow an action, and you reap a habit; sow a habit, and you reap a character; sow a character, and you reap a destiny." These are words that have the power to change the course of our lives.

Strategic thinking is way to process information mentally that leads to strategic planning. A strategy is a well-thought-out design for action. Before you can develop your plan of action, you have to develop your thoughts for that plan. The plan comes out of your thinking. That's why it is essential, as you follow your path to becoming a millionaire, that you get your mindset ready. Think of it this way. What you are about to do will come out of that brain in your head that sits on your shoulders. You cannot afford to proceed into the process without that brain ready to do the work effectively.

A study of the brain, and the research with brain scans, have helped us understand and use the brain more efficiently, revealing that different topics of thought happen in different parts of the brain. Most of us become focused on one area or topic in life and use little else of our brain. If you know how the brain works, you can use it to your advantage. So learn how the brain works. All the research is there, waiting for you to read online, for free.

Further studies have been done to show that getting a group of people together from different sectors of a business or manufacturing plant is like opening one whole brain. As the various people share their ideas, their views in their skill area, a whole picture emerges. But what if you are the only person currently in your business? How do you get your brain to function like a whole team? How do you get your whole brain activated?

There is a phrase, not attributed to anyone specifically, that describes stagnant thinking as "analysis paralysis." It means that a person who uses only a small part of the brain, which is most of us, cannot get past the same old thinking and doing things in the same old way. Most millionaires have figured out how to use most of their brain and the more you practice, the better you become at it. Eventually it is a habit and you don't have to work at it. This is directly connected with what has been discussed as the mindset of the millionaire, or the characteristics you need to develop to become a millionaire.

That is why it is so important to get yourself together and ready to think like a millionaire at the beginning. The sooner you get your head together, the sooner you will produce the wealth you anticipate. Strategic thinking will automatically become your mode of operation and strategic planning will, eventually, become a natural occurrence for you. When you get to that place, you are on your way. More than half the battle in thinking like a millionaire is getting your head in the game. Take that seriously and you will be successful.

The Brain of a Millionaire: The funny thing is that the brain of a millionaire is not any different from that of anybody else's brain. It comes down to how you use that brain in processing information. This is where a study of brain research comes in. The brain is divided into two main sides, four main quadrants and that's where thinking happens. There are other sections. The lower back operates our vision, the frontal lobe supports executive decision making, and so on. We cannot change the way we see without an appliance like glasses. Nor can we work and change the way we hear. Our brain also produces chemicals, which can be altered by diet and exercise to some extent, though there are people who have such a chemical imbalance, medication is required.

The good news is we can change the way we process information. There is a whole part of the brain where all of that happens and we use very little, often merely 20 percent. If you understand a few facts, you will be more apt to develop some changes. Your brain basically does two things with information. It receives it, and it expresses it. That happens in various ways. We receive information through our senses. We see, hear, feel, taste, and smell the world around us, and our nervous system transmits all that information to our brain. It is processed and stored there. On the other hand, we also express information. We usually speak, though we can express ourselves through motion, touch, a look, etc. If you know about Montessori schools, you know that they are based on the fact that learning is done best when all mods of our senses are awakened. Incoming information is processed more effectively, and in smarter ways, when you get it from more than one sensory mode. Translate that to thinking like a millionaire, and you become aware that merely listening to someone, or something, is enhanced if you have a visual to go with it; and you can even further entrench it into your mind if you are given a chance to voice it aloud. When you can't think of a word or phrase you want to use, talk to yourself about it aloud and you will find that your brain more easily recalls it. If your sense of smell is aroused during receptive language, more of your brain is activated. Use what research has made clear.

Many people know they learn better when there is music or a television going in the background, but they never thought about why. Some people like to toss a ball or think better shooting baskets. It is because it keeps more parts of your brain activated. Some people will learn better if the information is associated with visual input. Others seem to do better if they are not visually stimulated externally, but are allowed to form pictures in their brain. This opens the same area, but with more activity, because you are producing the picture, as opposed to just looking at one.

How often do your feel the need to touch something to get a better idea of what it is about? There are theories that people have different learning styles or modes. They say you are a visual learner or an auditory learner. The idea, though, that a visual person needs to have everything visual, or can only learn with visual props, is missing the point. If your visual processing is stronger, then use it, but work on development of the other parts of the brain. The more processes you activate, the more strategically effective your thinking will become.

To develop the thinking of a millionaire, you have to think strategically. That means finding ways to open your whole brain. Some people find that lying prone and closing their eyes brings a flood of ideas that are totally creative. If you've ever hear the phrase, "thinking outside of the box," you can understand that it means out of your fall back mode of processing. To shake up your brain, you have to be intentional. Go for a walk, listen to music, use scented lotion, or light a scented candle. Read something way out of your interest, watch a movie that is not normally your choice. Do things in a different order. Don't let yourself fall into a static place mentally. Do some artwork, learn to play an instrument, take a course in Japanese, or whatever it takes to get your whole brain moving and working in different ways. The payoff will be great. It is what creativity is all about. Creative people have learned to take risks, step out, be independent, and buck the system. Their brains are fully active most of the time.

What does strategic thinking really mean? Thinking strategically leads to strategic planning and action. You now understand how to wake up your brain, be more creative in your thinking so the next step is to exercise your brain processing on a regular basis. As you do, you will find yourself developing ideas or thoughts that are far to the right or left of your "normal." That's a good thing. That means you are moving toward thinking like a millionaire. Don't stop now. Your next step is to simply spend time reflecting or thinking about what you are doing, where you are going, and how you will get there, all using the whole brain. When you give time and importance to this task and open your whole mind, you will begin to see different paths to work around problems, and to progress toward your goals. You will eventually be able to see problems before they happen as your imagination is unleashed and you allow your brain to be free flowing. When people get together for brainstorming sessions it, in essence, is an activity that begins to push people to look at another way of thinking, and opens the minds of all to be more creative. Each person spurs the other on. But you can do this by yourself, if you are willing to work at it.

Interested in learning more? Why not take an online Habits of Millionaires course?

When your thinking is free to develop a wide spread of ideas, you are thinking strategically. Again, you have to be intentional about making time to reflect, evaluate, and plan in your mind. Only then are you ready to put your thoughts on paper, bounce them off someone else, and do some research to see if any of those ideas are plausible. This activity of thinking has to become a natural part of your rhythm, your mindset, and your characteristics. You are continuing to shape yourself into thinking like a millionaire.

Moving from strategic thinking to strategic planning: As you begin to think strategically, you may take notes, or not. You may speak your ideas into a tape recorder. You don't want to lose these creative thoughts and don't depend upon remembering them. Your natural mode will try to close off that creative activity, and you will lose it. When you have done it for years, your mind will learn to stay open all the time. For now use a note pad you can carry around with you or use your smart device, but get it down. You won't at first, thinking you will remember; but after forgetting several good ideas, you will learn to jot them down.

It is so easy when you want to accomplish great things to want to get out a chart and develop a strategy, a plan of action. Don't do it. Make yourself take several days to open your mind and just think creatively. You will be so surprised at how much better your plans will be. Then when you have put your plans on paper, you will notice that there are things you didn't think of. Go and think some more, and then go back to the plan. Think of it like a chess game. Begin to see the next few moves ahead and anticipate all the possible results of each move.

A PLAN OF ACTION FOR MONEY

Planning, reflection, evaluation, adjusting is all part of the process of a business that is aimed at success, however you might define that success. Don't skip parts of the process, or you will revert back to your old ways, your old habits, and your old ways of thinking. Your business will suffer if this happens. Be alert to slipping up in small ways. Have someone close at hand who is there just to keep you accountable to your own decisions. Check yourself often. Look in the mirror. There is a song from The Muppet Movie called "Am I a man or a Muppet?" You want to be a Muppet. Muppets are accepted for their off-the-wall ways.

Getting your plans down on paper or on a computer chart is important, but only when your mind is ready. Don't start down an important road without having the necessary tools. You don't have to be perfect at all of this, but you need to be pretty strong. If you start toward planning with bad habits, lack of energy, or without doing your research, it will take you twice as long to reach that target and it is probable that you won't reach it at all. You will meet with frustration and wonder what you did wrong.

Your plan needs to be where you can see it at all times. Actually putting it on chart paper and taping it up on a wall is not a bad idea. Throughout the day or night, you may have an idea that you want to put on the chart for consideration later. Don't let any idea get lost.

Summary: Strategic planning requires strategic thinking. Strategic thinking means thinking smart. To make this happen, you have to understand how your brain processes information. It will help you to work smarter if you are able to open up your whole brain. Figure out how to open your brain. What frees up your thinking? Develop a habit of using all of your senses, as often as you can; talk to yourself, draw pictures, listen to music, or lie down. When you figure out what works for you, go with it for a while, but switch it up before your brain becomes complacent again. Get outside your comfort zone in different ways. Read a strange book, go to a concert that you would not normally attend, or start a new hobby, like growing indoor succulents. The point is to jump into the deep end and wake your brain up.

Once you are thinking effectively or strategically, you will be ready to plan. Your plan is putting the goals in order as steps and ideas that you want to pursue. It will resemble a pathway full of goals and the action needed to reach those goals. Don't worry about putting it into a nice computerized chart. Just put it simply, on big chart paper so you can adjust it at when you see something you did not think of before. Get others to look it over and give you their ideas. You don't have to use them but it might awaken a new line of thought for you. Don't get set and be afraid to move things around, try something new, break out of your mold, or derive a new path. The more creative you get, the closer you will get to that million dollars.

When you get your plan down, work hard to make it happen -- learn and study along the way, discover new things, and broaden your world. Travel, join a club, or take a class and keep yourself involved physically and mentally with whatever is beyond your door. You have to know what people are thinking about, what they are using, what their problems are and to be an entrepreneur who is always growing and expanding the business. If you want your business to stay small, there is nothing wrong with that, but if you want to make millions of dollars, you are going to have to look into the future and read the tea leaves.

Example: Senait had an idea to invent a new kitchen tool. She fashioned a prototype from another tool, applied for a patent, and took it to a local manufacturer to see how he might make it. She worked with him until they had it perfected, but the cost to make it was too much. Senait went home to think. She spent several days thinking while she went for walks, listened to music, and went to visit a nursing home, taking some flowers from her garden. She began to get some ideas about how she might be able to make the tool cheaper. She made a list and then researched some of those ideas. As she researched, she had some friends over who were willing to discuss her ideas.

One of them remembered something from her past, when she had been overseas, that seemed to resonate with Senait. Senait began corresponding with a French chef about her invention, and as she did, she made still more changes. He invited her to visit, and she did. The chef was so impressed with her idea, he offered to let her use his name in her marketing. She offered him a royalty on each one sold once in production. It was a win-win situation. He recommended a manufacturer that made most of his tools and got her in to see the owner.

From there, she got a small business loan to fund the first production and set up her web store taking orders. It wasn't long before stores that sold kitchen supplies from all over the world were in contact with her and ordering. She began to think about diversifying, by using her brand to produce other kitchen products that she improved upon.

Consider this:

1. Any planning you do for your business, to become rich, or to develop a product, will rarely succeed if there is not strategic thinking before the planning. Action without thinking is never a good thing.

2. A quick online study of current brain research is free for the reading, as so much learning is on the Internet. Use what is available to you without costs. You are building equity in yourself.

3. If everyone activated their whole brain, the world would be full of very creative people.

4. If you activate your whole brain, you might be able to accomplish more at your job, in your career, and be able to demand a higher salary.

5. Everything it takes to become a millionaire is free for the taking; opportunity, learning, being creative, and living frugally. It's all about the choices you make each day.

Have you wondered how millionaires work on multiple businesses? How do they find time to work on so many major tasks making progress successfully? What exactly is their action plan for their success?

you will take the first step towards your dream goal. The idea isn't about completing a huge task. It is all about getting started no matter how small. Once you get the ball rolling, you will notice major progress on your goals in no time.

You will realize how millionaires make constant progress towards their goals with an action plan. Once you realize the importance of an action plan, you will know how to make steady progress towards your goals.

Since you are here, you must have woken up earlier today. Pat yourself on the back because you are already way ahead of the majority. Most people do not even get to the first step of taking the first step towards their goal.

You are unlike those people who live their life in mediocrity. You are one among those determined to live the life of your dreams, which you surely will if you consistently make progress like you have been doing so far.

Here is the biggest reason why millionaires make progress towards their goals. The reason is far more simpler than you think it is.

Millionaires achieve what they achieve by simply doing things.

They do not wait for the right time, the best time or a future time. They break a bigger goal into smaller tasks and get going with it.

As simple as it sounds, this is the main reason why millionaires are far ahead of the rest in terms of their goals.

The reason why you have no action plan towards your goal

Take a few moments to ponder why you haven't made any progress towards your long term goal.

Pause here right now. Spend a minutes thinking about the problems preventing you from working towards your dream goal.

In all likelihood, your "problems" will be among the following:

You do not have enough money to work towards your goal

You are too busy and do not have enough time to work towards your goal

The situation is not ideal currently to work towards your dream goal

Starting a few weeks/months later is the best time to begin

Guess what? All the elite successful people had the same set backs with one subtle difference. They did not look at them as problems to begin work at all.

Sure, some of them were indeed problems that they did not have a solution to. However, that did not stop them from beginning work. They believed they will work out a solution through the journey.

Take a look back at your problem to work towards your long term goal. It is usually a reason to avoid commencing work on your long term goal than a real problem in reality.

There is just one major differentiator between millionaires and the ordinary. The millionaires begin work on their long term goals while the ordinary don't. It is as simple as that.The difficulties faced and the skills possessed between the two groups are rarely significantly different. It is in the mindset where the bigger difference lies.

Since this is your dream that you are working towards, aren't you excited? If you are not very excited, you should revisit and answer the 3 questions to identify your long term goal. If you have your long term goals already, do consider setting them up as SMART Goals.

So, how can you begin your journey towards your long term goal? If you think again, you do not need any guidance on what you need to do this morning. Guess why?

You already have created the list of things that you need to do to achieve your goal when you broke down your goals into smaller chunks. In the exercise of creating your short term goals you had broken down your goal into tasks for this week, month and quarter. If you landed on this article directly.

What exactly you do does not really matter on this first day of your journey. What matters is that you ensure you take at least one step forward towards your goal today.

CHAPTER TWO

WHAT IS YOUR MONEY BLUPRINT

Whether I'm appearing on radio or television, I'm well-known for making the following statement: "Give me five minutes, and I can predict your financial future for the rest of your life." WEALTH PRINCIPLE: Give me five minutes, and I can predict your financial future for the rest of your life. How? In a short conversation, I can identify what's called your money and success "blueprint." Each of us has a per-sonal money and success blueprint already embedded in our subconscious mind. And this blueprint, more than anything and everything else combined, will determine your financial destiny. What is a money blueprint? As an analogy, let's consider the blueprint for a house, which is a preset plan or design for that particular home. In the same way, your money blueprint is simply your preset program or way of being in relation to money. I want to introduce you to an extremely important formula. It determines how you create your reality and wealth. Many of the most respected teachers in the field of human potential have used this formula as a foundation for their teachings. Called the Process of Manifestation, it goes like this: TAFAA = R WEALTH PRINCIPLE: Thoughts lead to feelings. Feelings lead to actions. Actions lead to results. Your financial blueprint consists of a combination of your thoughts, feelings, and actions in the arena of money. So how is your money blueprint formed? The answer is simple. Your financial blueprint consists primarily of the information or "programming" you received in the past, and especially as a young child. Who were the primary sources of this programming or conditioning? For most people, the list includes parents, sib-lings, friends, authority figures, teachers, religious leaders, media, and your culture, to name a few. Let's take culture. Isn't it true that certain cultures have one way of thinking and dealing with money, while other cultures have a different approach? Do you think a child comes out of the womb with his or her attitudes toward money, or do you believe the child is taught how to deal with money? That's right. Every child is taught how to think about and act in relation to money. The same holds true for you, for me, for everyone. You were taught how to think and act when it comes to money. These teachings become your conditioning, which becomes automatic responses that run you for the rest of your life. Unless, of course, you intercede and revise your mind's money files. This is exactly what we are going to do in this book, and what we do for thousands of people each year, on a deeper and more permanent level at the Millionaire Mind Intensive Seminar. We said earlier that thoughts lead to feelings, that feelings lead to actions, that actions lead to results. So here's an interesting question: Where do your thoughts come from? Why do you think differently from the next person? Your thoughts originate from the "files of information" you have in the storage cabinets of your mind. So where does this information come from? It comes from your past programming. That's right, your past conditioning determines every thought that bubbles up in your mind. That's why it's often referred to as the conditioned mind. money consistently there or was the flow more sporadic? Did money come easily in your family, or was it always a struggle? Was money a source of joy in your household or the cause of bitter arguments? Why is this information important? You've probably heard the saying "Monkey see, monkey do." Well, humans aren't far behind. As kids, we learn just about everything from modeling. Although most of us would hate to admit it, there's more than a grain of truth in the old saying "The apple doesn't fall too far from the tree." This reminds me of the story about a woman who prepares a ham for dinner by cutting off both ends. Her bewildered husband asks why she cuts off the ends. She replies, "That's how my mom cooked it." Well, it just so happened that her mom was coming for dinner that night. So they asked her why she cut off the ends of the ham. Mom replies, "That's how my mom cooked it." So they decide to call Grandma on the phone and ask why she cut off the ends of the ham. Her answer? "Because my pan was too small!" The point is that generally speaking, we tend to be identical to one or a combination of our parents in the arena of money.

For example, my dad was an entrepreneur. He was in the home-building business. He built anywhere from a dozen to a hundred homes per project. Each project took a huge amount of capital investment. My dad would have to put up everything we had and borrow heavily from the bank until the homes were sold and the cash came through. Consequently, at the beginning of each project, we had no money and were in debt up to our eyeballs. As you can imagine, during this period my dad was not in the best of moods nor was generosity his strong suit. If I asked him for anything that cost even a penny, his standard reply after the usual "What am I, made of money?" was "Are you crazy?" Of course, I wouldn't get a dime, but what I would get was that "Don't even think of asking again" glare. I'm sure you know the one.

MONEY BLUPRINT

This scenario would last for about a year or two until the homes were finally sold. Then, we'd be rolling in dough. All of a sudden, my dad was a different person. He'd be happy, kind, and extremely generous. He'd come over and ask me if I needed a few bucks. I felt like giving him his glare back, but I wasn't that stupid so I just said, "Sure, Dad, thanks," and rolled my eyes. Life was good... until that dreaded day when he'd come home and announce, "I found a good piece of land. We're going to build again." I distinctly remember saying, "Great, Dad, good luck," as my heart sank, knowing the struggle that was about to unfold again. This pattern lasted from the time I could remember, when I was about six, until the age of twenty-one, when I moved out of my parents' house for good. Then it stopped, or so I thought. At twenty-one years of age, I finished school and became, you guessed it, a builder. I then went on to several other types of project-based businesses. For some strange reason, I'd make a small fortune, but just a short time later, I'd be broke. I'd get into another business and believe I was on top of the world again, only to hit bottom a year later. This up-and-down pattern went on for nearly ten years before I realized that maybe the problem wasn't the type of business I was choosing, the partners I was choosing, the employees I had, the state of the economy, or my decision to take time off and relax when things were going well. I finally recognized that maybe, just maybe, I was unconsciously reliving my dad's up-and-down income pattern.

CHAPTER THREE

PATHS TO WEALTH BUILDING

There's no mystery to becoming a millionaire. Anyone can do it. Take, for example, the unassuming utility company maintenance man making a modest salary over a 36-year period. He lived below his means, even buying clothes at thrift shops, yet enjoyed watercolor painting, ballroom dancing, traveling, and investing. And left $3 million in stocks and real estate to charities. Or the copier salesman in a small town who took over a small store of his own. He worked seven days a week, took few vacations, raised two children, bought some real estate, and invested the maximum in retirement savings. At age 41 he sold the shop for $1 million and continued working for the new owners. Or the doctor who raised four kids and still managed to retire with almost $2 million. And how about all those steady American workers—schoolteachers, city librarians, police officers, nurses, and lab techs—who retire on a nice combination of resources from a pension, 401(k), Social Security, a few stocks, bonds, and funds, a low mortgage, and some real estate? The Only Real Way to Become a Millionaire Actually, the most difficult step on the road to becoming a millionaire is the first step. And the first step is not just "getting started," as most experts will tell you (although that's a big one). The first step is making sure you're pointed the right way—your way. Most people aren't! Most people have trouble getting started because they haven't figured out which way is their way. All too many people are headed in the wrong direction, going nowhere fast. Or they arrive in the wrong place too late, traveling somebody else's path. Or, frustrated, they give up before they even get started. And that's what this Millionaire's Personality Code is all about, helping you discover the only real way you can ever become a millionaire— your way. There's no big mystery about how to become a millionaire. You can easily find tons of information in libraries, bookstores, periodicals, and online. So here's the big question for you: If we have all this fancy ultrasophisticated information, why are there are so darn few millionaires in America? Why are there only 8 million in a nation of 283 million people? That's less than 4 percent of the population. Very simple—the reason there aren't more millionaires in America is not because you and I lack the information. We know we have all the formulas, tools, databases, newsletters, methodologies, and software we'll ever need on budgeting, saving, investing, and all the other tricks essential to becoming a millionaire. The problem is, we have too @#%& much information, not too little! Looking for Love in All the Wrong Places You have all the books and magazines you'll ever need telling you exactly how to follow some simple set of rules or steps, even guaranteeing that if you do you'll become a millionaire and retire happy as a clam. But in this new age of information overload, all the formulas, rules, and steps go in one ear and out the other, as my grandpa used to say. Our attention span rapidly fades. For so many of us, the cookie-cutter formulas don't feel right—so we're off looking for the next new book, hoping it will fit who we are. That's right, as wonderful as it all sounds, most investors tune out most of the information because somehow—no matter how good things look on paper in that book or magazine—it just doesn't fit your personality! Why 90 Percent Are Going in the Wrong Direction So, what's the problem? The problem is that there really is no one-sizefits-all, cookie-cutter approach to becoming a millionaire. As a result, the vast majority of Americans trying to become millionaires are doing it the wrong way—doing it someone else's way, using formulas that just don't fit with their true personality. Or worse yet, they get frustrated, give up, and do nothing. No wonder we have so few millionaires. Studies by such respected organizations such as the American Association for Retired Persons (AARP), Employee Benefit Research Institute (EBRI), Economic Policy Institute (EPI), Consumer Federation of America, and the U.S. Bureau of Economic Analysis tell us that only one in three Americans are saving enough to retire comfortably and that the average American's portfolio is less than $100,000 at retirement, including home equity. Many Americans may never be able to retire, let alone become millionaires. Wall Street's Not Your Friend Wall Street's money managers have most Americans believing that Wall Street gurus can beat the market and that you can't win without their superior intelligence. Wall Street spends over $15 billion annually for marketing and advertisements to keep you dependent on this illusion. Yes, it's a big hoax:

Several research studies confirm, for example, that Wall Street's actively managed mutual funds charge excessive loads and higher fees, even though Wall Street firms consistently underperform the top no-load funds run by an independent fund company like Vanguard. No wonder Wall Street hates to see books come along like The Four Pillars of Investing, in which Dr. William Bernstein, a neurologist and money manager, bluntly says that Wall Street operates with the "ethics of Bonny and Clyde," and they do it under the cloak of legitimacy, disguised as a trusted friend. Yet study after study consistently proves that Wall Street's money managers charge more for their services and return less to investors. The fact is, Wall Street money managers don't give a hoot about you personally. Oh, they will smile and pretend, but Wall Street's primary goal is to increase assets under management and gain control of your money so they can charge higher account fees and expenses, book more earnings, and increase profit margins—at your expense. You can do better without Wall Street. Yes, You Are Unique—Trust That Still Small Voice The problem goes back to the culture of Wall Street and the entire financial services industry, including fund companies, cable news networks, and best-selling gurus, magazine writers, and newspaper editors. Like sheep, they go along with the Wall Street myth, either focusing on one-size-fits-all, cookie-cutter approaches to getting rich and becoming a millionaire, or confusing the issue with lots of information so that Main Street will, by default, turn to Wall Street for advice. Occasionally, however, a still small voice will scream inside your head "But wait, I'm unique." And you're right—you are unique. Your brain is wired differently. Your DNA and your genes point you in a special direction, down a road less traveled that's off the beaten path—and on your path. It should come as no surprise that you'll naturally resist all the mechanical how-to formulas you've read over and over again in Borders and Barnes & Noble. Find the Path Made for Your Unique Personality That's where The Millionaire Code comes in. This book is designed to help you understand why you're different (and why it's okay to be different!) and to help you discover the only real way you can ever become a millionaire—your way. There is no one-size-fits-all, cookie-cutter formula to becoming a millionaire. None. Life would be less of a struggle if there were. But as we all discover sooner or later, what worked for your father or mother, for your siblings or best friend, is probably wrong for you. Even what your wellintentioned teachers, mentors, coaches, or favorite uncle think is best for you may be wrong. In fact, research studies show that the vast majority of college graduates aren't working in their major field of study. Moreover, studies show that most graduates will make at least three career changes in their lifetime. Like it or not—you've got to find the path that fits you and you alone. To Thy Own Self Be True—Period! The only real mystery—if there is one—is discovering the real you and the millionaire within you. We've heard this great challenge so often since ancient times. Writing in the Tao Te Ching 5,000 years ago, Lao Tzu tells us to "follow your true nature." Twenty-five hundred years ago, Plato repeated the message: "Know thyself." Down though the ages, great mystics of all faiths tell us to "listen to the still, small voice within," for there lies the truth of our being. Get in touch with the real you and your mission in life—and then your unique path to getting rich in spirit and in fact will become obvious. You can avoid the false starts and increase your odds of becoming a millionaire by first identifying your unique personality code—yes first, before you start saving and investing and all the rest of the stuff you need to do to accumulate a million bucks. Know your code, and get into action, and you'll join a powerful yet quiet subculture in pursuit of the new American Dream—retiring as a millionaire. Statistically, we know there are already 8 million millionaires in America. That's about 3.6 percent of the total population of 283 million people. Some experts predict the number will grow to as many as 50 million American millionaires by 2025. That means that today we could have as many as 42 million Americans on the path to retiring as millionaires. Of course, inflation will have some impact on the results. But however you look at it, there are roughly 42 million millionaires in training in America today, searching for the best way to capture this new American Dream.

PATH OF WEALTH

What's the best way for you? It's probably not what your boss says you're great at. Not something that's one of the latest top 20 hot career fields in America. Probably not something you score well on in some standard tests. And it's likely not even the job you've been doing for a few too many years: • Shifting into high gear: You could be one of the 35 percent of Americans who are already building a nest egg—but you just want to accelerate things and retire early. • Running on empty: Maybe you're doing all the right stuff (at least what seemed like the right stuff years ago). You're making a good living, but you're unhappy with your life and feeling as though you've been wasting time in the wrong career. • Happy, but broke: Maybe you are doing exactly what you want to do, perhaps fulfilling your life's mission helping the handicapped, but you're not making much money, or you'd just like to find ways to better fund the work. At least we can help confirm that you're doing the right thing. • Still searching: More likely, you're one of the 65 percent of Americans who really aren't doing much about becoming a millionaire, very possibly because you haven't discovered the real you, your mission in life, the millionaire within. Whatever the case, something tells you it's time to get in touch with your secret millionaire's personality code, time to get in sync with your true self, time to get in the millionaire's spirit, now, today.

CHAPTER FOUR

5 SECRETS REVELED

1. Make Your Life Happy Before Making a Million One of the key things I learned during these many interviews is that you need to make your life happy FIRST. That doesnt mean being rich or working towards a million. That means working on the other aspects of your life. Everyone thinks the million will give us the lives we want. I can tell you after interviewing 120 millionaires, it doesnt.If you want an enjoyable life, its easier to obtain that enjoyable life first – before making your first million. It can still be about the money, but only after you choose your life. ūAfter you become a millionaire, you can give all of your money away because whatŨs important is not the million dollars; whatŨs important is the person you have become in the process of becoming a millionaire.Ŭ – Jim Rohn Action Item: Evaluate your life and change one thing youre not happy with. Take a good, hard look at your life. Certainly there are things you would want to change. Choose one thing youre not happy with – maybe its the lack of time you spend with friends and family, maybe its a lack of self-care. Whatever it is, name it and find a way to change it so you can be happy. Changing just one thing will have a profound effect on your life as a whole. 2. Control Your Money (Dont Let It Control You) Millionaires set a goal and then work toward it. Theres never a nebulous plan for a million. One of the first steps in that plan is often to get rid of your debts and take control.Debts have a nasty habit of controlling you and you have to take control of them before you can ever achieve bigger financial goals! Next, work on your lifestyle. Figure out what work makes you happy by trying different things. A helpful homework assignment is to write down what your perfect day would look like. This will give you an idea of what will truly make you happy. As Harvards resident happiness professor, Tal Ben-Shahar told Yes Magazine.org: ūHappiness lies at the intersection between pleasure and meaning. Whether at work or at

home, the goal is to engage in activities that are both personally significant and enjoyable.Ŭ Once youve made your work and life happy, NOW you can work on the big money. Figure out what your real goal is, whether its to create a million dollar business or just have enough money to retire comfortably. Then start to work toward that goal. Remember, your goal should be your own and not just a vague goal of having a certain amount of money. Its not all about the money and your goal should reflect that. While your final goal will definitely include money, it should also include other things important to YOU – to be the goal to achieve. Action Item: Create a debt repayment plan and follow through with it. List all of your debts and their minimum monthly payments. Figure out how much extra you can pay on the debt. Put that extra amount toward the smallest debt or the debt with the highest interest rate and set them all on automatic monthly payments. Once that first debt is repaid, take the entire amount you were paying on that first debt and add it to the minimum payment of the next debt to accelerate that payoff. This is known as the debt snowball method and you can use this free calculator to make the math easy. Follow this plan until the debt is gone. 3. Take Opportunities Millionaires constantly rise to meet any challenge presented to them. When an opportunity falls into their lap, they take it, barreling through any obstacles that might be in the way. Millionaires dont sit around for weeks analyzing an opportunity or making excuses for why they cant follow through with it. They do whatever it takes to meet the challenge and do it well. This is an important trait of all millionaires and a mindset you should adopt if you want to become one. The point is opportunities, especially the great ones, dont come very often.Therefore, when an opportunity arises, you have to take it no matter what, providing you have the confidence to turn this opportunity into a win for yourself. Action Item: Say yes to at least one new opportunity. When a new opportunity arises, say yes, even if its scary or something youve never done. This might be an invitation to speak at a conference, a guest blogging opportunity, or something else. No matter what it is, make it a point to say yes. 4. Overcome Your Excuses Speaking of excuses, millionaires dont let excuses hold them back from anything. They realize every excuse has a solution and they work hard to find the solution to every excuse that may arise. They take action, any action – no matter how small. If you want something bad enough then youll undoubtedly find a way around any excuse you can come up with. As they say, where theres a will, theres a way.

Millionaires live by this code.

SECRETS REVELED OF THE MONEY

If youre someone who wishes to become a millionaire, then you have to live by this code, too. You can start with small things and see whether you can get around excuses. The more you do it, the easier it will become. This is a very important step because getting past excuses results in you becoming less and less indolent with time. This creates a strong work ethic and produces greater results. Action Item: Identify one excuse youve been using as a crutch and take action to squash it. Think about all the excuses you make in a day. Do you ever say, I dont have time for.., or I would do that, but...? These are excuses that dont help you move forward. Identify one of your more frequent excuses and find a way to overcome it and make that thing happen. If you feel you dont have time for something, take action by prioritizing your time and making room for that one thing.

5. Millionaires Play a Bigger Game Finally, Ive noticed how things that seem huge or scary to me are old hat to millionaires. This is because they take those scary steps in order to keep moving forward. The more we do things, the more normal they get. For example, when I first started my site, I was a nervous wreck about interviewing millionaires. But now that Ive been

doing it for so long, Im totally used to it. Its old hat for me. The same can be true for you with that thing youre scared of doing. When you think about the most famous millionaires, there are a few words that probably come to mind, and one of these words is usually fearless. Thats because when they have a fear of doing something, theyre brave enough to overcome it, plow through it, and see their plan come to fruition. Action Item: Do one thing youve been too scared to try and just do it. What have you been putting off because youre afraid of failing (or maybe afraid of succeeding)? Name it and put it on the calendar. This gives you a goal and a deadline. Once you do it, youll wonder why you were ever afraid to do it in the first place.

Five years ago we began studying how people become wealthy. Initially, we did it just as you might imagine, by surveying people in so-called upscale neighborhoods across the country. In time, we discovered something odd. Many people who live in expensive homes and drive luxury cars do not actually have much wealth. Then, we discovered something even odder: Many people who have a great deal of wealth do not even live in upscale neighborhoods.

Why are so many people interested in what we have to say? Because we have discovered who the wealthy really are and who they are not. And, most important, we have determined how ordinary people can become wealthy. What is so profound about these discoveries? Just this: Most people have it all wrong about wealth in India. Wealth is not the same as income. If you make a good income each year and spend it all, you are not getting wealthier. You are just living high. Wealth is what you accumulate, not what you spend. How do you become wealthy? Here, too, most people have it wrong. It is seldom luck or inheritance or advanced degrees or evenintelligence that enables people to amass fortunes. Wealth is more often the result of a lifestyle of hard work, perseverance, planning, and, most of all, self-discipline.Many people ask this question of themselves all the time. Often they are hard-working, welleducated, high-income people. Why, then, are so few affluent?

CHAPTER FIVE

MILLIONAIRE GAME

TRUE OR FALSE? 1. Most millionaires are college graduates. TRUE 2. Most millionaires work fewer than 40 hours a week. FALSE 3. More than half of all millionaires never received money from a trust fund or estate. TRUE 4. More millionaires have American Express Gold Cards than Sears cards. FALSE 5. More millionaires drive Fords than Cadillacs. TRUE 6. Most millionaires work in glamorous jobs, such as sports, entertainment, or high tech. FALSE 7. Most millionaires work for big Fortune 500 companies. FALSE 8. Many poor people become millionaires by winning the lottery. FALSE 9. College graduates earn about 65% more than high school graduates earn. TRUE 10. If an average 18-year-old high school graduate spends as much as an average high school dropout until both are 67 years old, but the high school graduate invests the difference in his or her earnings at 8% annual interest, the high school graduate would have $5,500,000. TRUE 11. Day traders usually beat the stock market and many of them become millionaires. FALSE 12. If you want to be a millionaire, avoid the risky stock market. FALSE 13. At age 18, you decide not to smoke and save $1.50 a day. You invest this $1.50 a day at 8% annual interest until you are 67. At age 67, your savings from not smoking are almost $300,000. TRUE 14. If you save $2,000 a year from age 22 to age 65 at 8% annual interest, your savings will be over $700,000 at age 65. TRUE 15. Single people are more often millionaires than married people. FALSE.

Millionaire Game

CHAPTER SIX

MAKE YOUR FINANCIAL PLAN AUTOMATIC! Put Your Money on Autopilot

Many Individuals aspire to become a millionaire, but only handful of them push themselves hard enough to achieve this goal. Today, when being a billionaire is the new focus for the wealthy, becoming a millionaire is a possibility for many, and it generally boils down to rational thinking and occasional calculated risks. Moreover, there are no tricks or scams involved in getting that millionaire tag, just good old-fashioned consistent and disciplined investing. If you are ready to invest smartly to reach your millionaire milestone, here are few steps to help you get there:

Start Saving a Percentage of Your Monthly Income

When you are young, it's hard to envision what life would be 30 after 35 years. There is additionally the peer pressure to have the most recent cell phone, wear elegant brands and drive the latest cars.Instead, start saving a percentage of your monthly income. You must save at least 10% of your monthly take-home income towards your goal to achieve your first millionaire milestone.

PUT YOUR FINANCES ON AUTOPILOT

Diversifying Your Investment Plans

While regular saving is important, it is equally important to invest in the right type of asset in order to actually achieve your first millionaire milestone.

It's simple! Select investments which can help you in the long-term. In this case, equity could become a preferred choice. You can also look at diversifying your investment amongst stocks, mutual funds, Unit Linked Insurance Plans (ULIP plans) etc.

Whatever investment option you choose, maintain a proper proportion of equity, debt and balanced funds, to prevent your portfolio from becoming too risky or too conservative. Unit Linked Insurance Plans (ULIP plan) perfectly fit this need.

ULIP plan allows you to choose funds of your choice, whether it's equity funds, debt funds or balanced funds and additionally allow you to switch between funds. This feature is particularly helpful when there is a need to switch the funds of your ULIP plan considering the ongoing market conditions.

Invest Diligently and Invest for Growth

As your wealth grows, you will have more and more investment opportunities available to you, so, accordingly increase your investment amount. You could begin by investing any additional gains like incentives or bonuses to prepone your target achievement.

However, managing your money can be time-consuming. So, once you develop your investment plan, arrange automatic periodic transfers from your bank account to the fund house or insurance company.

Review Your Investment Once A Year

Your work does not end at investing alone. You should continually review your investment, at least once a year, no more no less. In case your fund has underperformed compared to its benchmark, investigate the reasons for the underperformance and the likelihood of persistence of these reasons in the future before deciding your course of action.

Even though converting savings of a couple of thousand rupees per month to 10 million rupees resembles a difficult or rather unachievable task, beginning early and having the correct approach make it doable.Hopefully breaking the first 10 million mark will ignite the fire in you, and you will find the next 10 million is accomplished quicker.

Wondering how to become a millionaire? It may sound impossible to some people, but it doesn't have to be an out-of-reach pipe dream. With careful planning, patience, and smart savings, you can easily make a million dollars by the time you retire.

If you want to become a millionaire, the most important thing you can do is to start early so you can take advantage of compounding.

Keep your spending in check. You'll have more money to save and invest and you'll reach your goal faster.

Max out your retirement accounts whenever possible, especially when your employer matches your contribution.

Having a million-dollar portfolio is a retirement dream for many people. Making that dream come true requires some serious effort. While success is never a sure thing, the 10 steps outlined below will go a long way toward helping you achieve your objective.

1. Set a Goal

Nobody plans to fail, but plenty of people fail to plan. It's a cliché, but it's true. Making a plan is the leading self-help advice from athletes, business moguls and everyday people who have achieved extraordinary goals.

KEY TAKEAWAYS

To retire as a millionaire, the first thing you need is a proper retirement plan for the long haul.

Employer-sponsored retirement accounts where your company matches your contributions are a great way to sock away cash.

Stick to your budget and spend within your means, avoiding debilitating credit card debt.

2. Start Saving

If you don't save, you'll never reach your goal. As obvious as this might seem, far too many people never even start to save. If your employer offers a 401(k) plan, enrolling in it is a great way to put your savings on auto-pilot. Simply sign up for the plan and contributions will be automatically taken out of your paycheck, increasing your savings and decreasing your immediate tax liability.

If your employer offers to match your contributions up to a certain percentage, be sure to contribute enough to get the full match. It's like getting a guaranteed return on your investment. Finding the cash to stash may be a challenge, particularly when you're young, but don't let that stop you from pursuing future riches. And remember that the younger you start, the more time your money has to grow.

If you want to become a millionaire, the most important thing you can do is to start early so you can take advantage of compounding.

Keep your spending in check. You'll have more money to save and invest and you'll reach your goal faster.

Max out your retirement accounts whenever possible, especially when your employer matches your contribution.

Get Aggressive

Take a hard look at your asset allocation. If you are looking to grow your wealth over time, fixed-income investments such as annuities, which offer fixed payments that can neither grow nor shrink, aren't likely to get the job done. Why? Because inflation can take a big chunk out of your savings.

Studies have shown that the majority of the returns generated by an investment are dictated by asset allocation. Investing in equities entails more risk, but is also statistically likely to lead to greater returns. For many of us, it's a risk we have to take if we want to see our wealth grow. Asset-allocation strategies can help you learn how to make picking the right mix of securities the core of your investing strategy.

Prepare for Rainy Days

Part of long-term planning involves accepting the idea that setbacks will occur. If you are not prepared, these setbacks can put a stop to your savings efforts. While you can't avoid all of the bumps in the road, you can prepare in advance to mitigate the damage they can do by always maintaining an emergency fund. This fund will also help keep you from building up credit card debt or prematurely tapping your retirement funds, two ways people pay for emergencies that can undercut their financial security.

Your income should rise as time passes. You'll get raises, change jobs, and maybe get married and become a two-income family. Every time your salary rises, so should the amount that you save. The key to reaching your goal as quickly as possible is to save as much as you can.

Watch Your Spending

Vacations, cars, kids, and all of life's other expenses take a big chunk out of your paycheck. To maximize your savings, you need to minimize your spending. Buying a home you can afford and living a lifestyle that is below your means and not funded by credit cards are necessities if you want to boost your savings.

Monitor Your Portfolio

There's no need to obsess over every movement of the Dow Jones Industrial Average. Instead, check your portfolio once a year. Rebalance your asset allocation to keep on track with your plan.

Max Out Your Options

Take advantage of every savings opportunity that comes your way. Make the maximum contribution to tax-deferred savings plans, then open up a taxable investment account, too.2

Don't let any chance to save get away.

Catch-Up Contributions

When you reach age 50, you are eligible to increase your contributions to tax-deferred savings plans. The IRS calls this a catch-up contribution.3 Make sure to take advantage of the opportunity.

Have Patience

Get-rich-quick schemes are usually just that—schemes. The power of compounding takes time, so invest early and often, and accept that the road to riches is often long and slow. With that in mind, the sooner you get started, the better your odds of achieving your goals.

Retirement might seem far away, but when it arrives nobody ever complains about having too much money. Some people even question whether a million is enough. Test that theory by figuring out whether your retirement income goal still makes sense. That said, with lots of planning and discipline, you can reach your retirement goals and live a comfortable life after work.

key is to put your Money on Autopilot

Automating your finances isn't rocket science, but it's still the best way to save more and worry less.

The most important factor in financial success is not having a budget, meticulously avoiding debt, or choosing the right investments. It is having a system that makes the right financial moves for you.

The decision to save money is both a personal and at the same times a financial decision. It's personal because you make the decision, and it's financial because you need to put away some money. Very often people find themselves stuck between what they are willing to do (i.e. save on a constant basis) and how to "execute" what they are willing to do.

Knowing that your paycheck is going to show up in your account on a specific day is good for your peace of mind and it saves you from having to make a trip to the bank. If your employer offers direct deposit, all it takes to sign up is filling out a form and providing your bank account information. You can even split up the deposit over several accounts. It's a good idea to send a certain amount of your pay straight to your savings so you don't have to go back and transfer it over later on.

Have you opened a savings account in the past, but forgot to actually add money into it on a regular basis? Sometimes the biggest barrier to saving money is simply remembering to do it. One option is to set up an automatic payment from your bank account into your savings account at the end of each month (or weekly, if you get paid every week).

But if you get paid inconsistently (for example, if you're a casual shift worker, contractor or freelancer) or your expenses change month to month, it can be hard to commit to a regular savings amount. Some banks offer tools that scan your bank account and savings account, and move money between each account depending on your capacity to save.

Sometime we do stupid stuff because we are emotional or tempted. And sometimes we're just lazy.

If you currently pay for a monthly subscription that you don't use a gym, a magazine, $12 a month for DVR service on cable and don't do anything about it, whose fault is it? The recurring-subscription business model that gyms, cable companies, and Netflix use is one of the most stable and profitable in existence. And guess what? It is built on the simple fact that people are lazy. When we stop using something, most people will pay $20 or more each month for many months before making a 10 minute phone call to cancel.Not many people get excited by the idea of creating a spreadsheet to manually track their spending and expenses. This is especially true if you're a self-confessed lazy person, like me. But in order to save money, you need to have a clear understanding of what you've got coming in and what's going out (and exactly where it's going). An easy way to do this is to use an app that automatically groups your transactions into categories for you. One way around this is to put the money someplace where it's a little harder to reach, like a separate, dedicated high-interest savings account, or maybe staggered CDs. If you have an IRA or other long-term investments with a financial firm, you might want to set up an automatic investment to a non-retirement account there.

Emotional decision-making is part of the problem; pure temptation is another. If you have ever tried to resist a temptation to turn down an extra drink, to surf YouTube instead of working, to buy something you shouldn't and failed, you know what I mean.

Psychologists have shows that although it is possible to stretch and strengthen our willpower like a muscle, our ability to self-regulate is a consumable resource that depletes.

As you get older, your finances will get more complicated whether you want them to or not. So the simpler you can keep your financial system, the better. Two primary accounts one checking and one savings should suffice unless you own a business or are married with separate finances.

Managing your money can be a source of stress and uncertainty.

When was that bill due? Am I saving enough for retirement? Did someone steal my credit card and use it to buy crypto-mining robots?

While some of the above concerns may be more realistic than others, you won't have to worry about any of them if you've properly automated your finances. That may sound like an advanced topic only accessible to computer geniuses, but it's actually easy for anyone with a phone and internet connection.

Don't believe me?

Technically, you don't need to automate your personal finances. Most banks and merchants will still let you do everything by mail or over the phone.

I imagine, however, that you have other things you'd rather be doing. And this is one of the main arguments for financial automation: it saves you time. Less time paying bills, moving money to investments, or calling your bank about potential fraud means more time for the things you enjoy.

Beyond that, automating your finances brings peace of mind. You don't have to worry in the middle of the night if your credit card information has been stolen. Instead, you can know you'll get a text alerting you to suspicious charges.

Finally, automating your money increases your financial security. A missed payment, for instance, can seriously damage your credit score. But if you have your bills set to be paid automatically, then your finances will remain healthy even while you sleep.

Automated bill pay has two huge advantages. First, it saves you time since you won't have to manually pay bills. And if that wasn't enough, it will protect your credit score (since you won't have to worry about late payments).

So what can/should you automate? While this isn't a complete list, here are some of the most common bills we recommend setting to autopay:

Rent

Utility bills

Credit card payments

Student loan payments

Car payments

Insurance premiums (renters, auto, home, etc.)

As far as how to automate each of these, you should check with the specific company or institution billing you. Usually, you just have to agree to the recurring charges and provide payment information.

This could take some time if you're currently paying all of your bills manually. But once you have everything set up, you barely have to think about it. The only necessary maintenance is to update your payment information if it changes.This tip assumes that you aren't spending more than you're making and are generally in a financially stable position. If you can't afford to pay your bills, then you should address that before setting them to be paid automatically.

While digital banking has made it much easier to manage all of your various accounts, that doesn't mean you have time to check each transaction every day.

Because of this, a fraudulent charge could slip through without you even noticing. Before you know it, your card will have racked up hundreds of dollars of charges at Taco Bells around the LA metro area. (This really happened with a card of mine years ago.)

If you have fraud alerts set up, however, then your financial institution will alert you the moment someone makes a suspicious charge to your card. You'll then need to confirm if the charge is valid. If it is, you can continue with your life as usual. But if it's not, then your financial institution can cancel the stolen card and send you a new one ASAP.

The details of setting up fraud alerts will vary, but you should be able to find the option in the "My Account" or "Security & Privacy" section of your financial institution's website or mobile app. You can also find instructions by searching "NAME OF YOUR BANK OR CREDIT CARD + fraud alerts".

One of the best ways to build credit responsibly is to only use your card for recurring charges such as a gym membership or streaming service. This way, you establish a consistent payment history without the temptation to overspend.

If/when your credit card information changes, however, it can be a pain to update all your various subscriptions.

That is, unless your online credit card account can show you a list of all your recurring charges and subscriptions. While not available with every card, it's worth seeing if yours offers it. I recently used it to update the subscriptions on my business credit card, and it vastly sped up the process.

If you've set up automatic bill pay and fraud alerts, then you can move on to automations that will help you retain or even make money. The first of these is automatic savings.

Automatically saving money has many advantages. First, it can be a great way to build up your emergency fund before you start investing. And beyond that, automatic monthly savings are a great way to amass the cash you need for large purchases such as a downpayment on a home.

The details of how to set up automatic withdrawals to savings will vary based on where you bank. But generally, you have the option to set up recurring withdrawals every 2 weeks, every month, or however often works best for you.

Ideally, you should set these withdrawals to happen each time you get paid. And the money should go into an account where you won't be tempted to spend it. Also, we recommend using the highest-interest savings account you can find.

Whatever you do, don't rely on your own memory, willpower, or motivation to save money. Set it up once and then forget about it.

CHAPTER SEVEN

HAPPINESS OF MILLIONAIRES

HAPPINESS OF MILLIONAIRES

Two samples of more than four thousand millionaires reveal two primary findings. First, only at high levels of wealth – in excess of $8 million (Study 1) and $10 million (Study 2) – are wealthier millionaires happier than millionaires with lower levels of wealth, though these differences are modest in magnitude. Second, controlling for total wealth, millionaires who have earned their wealth are moderately happier than those who inherited it. Taken together, these results suggest that, among millionaires, wealth may be likely to pay off in greater happiness only at very high levels of wealth, and when that wealth was earned rather than inherited.The Amount and Source of Millionaires' Wealth (Moderately) Predicts Their Happiness Many people aspire to great wealth, and becoming a millionaire is a commonly used reference for financial success (Kasser & Ryan, 1993); moreover, people tend to think that more money is related to more happiness (Aknin, Norton, & Dunn, 2009; Myers, 2000a). But does great wealth bring great happiness? If so, how much wealth is required? And, does the manner in which that wealth is accrued – whether you earned it yourself, or inherited it – predict the amount of happiness experienced? We use two large and unique samples of millionaires to shed novel light on these fundamental questions about the relationship between money and happiness. A large body of cross-sectional survey research demonstrates that overall life satisfaction continues to rise with income, though typically with diminishing marginal return (e.g., Aknin et al., 2009; Kahneman & Deaton, 2010; Myers, 2000b; Stevenson & Wolfers, 2008). However, the vast majority of the data informing our understanding of this relationship is derived from samples that have relied heavily on average earners (e.g., Cummings, 2000) and the poor (Biswas-Diener & Diener, 2006). For instance, Cummings (2000) meta-analytically reviewed effect sizes from 31 studies that investigated the relation between subjective wellbeing and income. Only one of these samples included individuals who made more than $150,000 annually. Additionally, many studies investigating the influence of wealth on happiness have utilized large panel data sets (e.g., Diener, Ng, Harter, & Arora, 2010; Kahneman & Deaton, 2010; Ng & Diener, 2014). These datasets, while large, are also typically representative of the sample populations and only identify a small number of "wealthy" participants as making over $150,000 a year. Further, many convenience samples (e.g., Aknin et al., 2009; Diener & Diener, 2009; Diener, Tay, & Oishi, 2013; Johnson & Krueger, 2006) are also missing data from wealthy individuals – likely because they are less likely to respond to requests to complete surveys (see Page, Bartels, & Seawright, 2013). Compounding this issue, comparisons of well-being at the individual level have relied primarily on personal or household annual income (e.g., Blanchflower & Oswald, 2004; Di Tella, Haisken-De New, & MacCulloch, 2010; Diener & Diener, 2009; Kahneman & Deaton, 2010), which typically has a more restricted range than people's net worth – which can be accumulated over time and includes all assets in addition to income (Headey & Wooden, 2004). A number of large panel data sets include a small proportion of participants who report a relatively high annual household income (datasets and proportion of sample with annual household income exceeding the top value listed in parentheses: the United States General Social Survey [12.6% over $110,000], the German Socio-Economic Panel [.67% over $120,000], the National Longitudinal Survey [.84% over $150,000], the United States National Survey of Midlife Development [6.07% over $150,000], and the Taiwan Social Change Survey [7.68% over $150,000]). These top income levels are much lower than the wealth levels in our samples, and these surveys do not break down these high income respondents into even smaller buckets of very high income respondents, such that there are not sufficient numbers of high net worth individuals to compare to our samples. In sum, previous analyses of the relationship between money and happiness have typically been subject to a restricted range problem – at the higher end in particular. One approach towards understanding the relationship between wealth and wellbeing among the wealthy has been to evaluate lottery winners. However, research on lottery wins has also failed to evaluate large samples of wealthy individuals, typically focusing on individuals who won small sums, with just a handful of "big winners." For instance Brickman, Coates and Janoff-Bulman (1978) compared 22 lottery winners (with average winnings of ~$480,000) to non-winners from the same geographical areas. Lottery winners were not found to be any happier than control participants, but did report taking less pleasure in ordinary activities (e.g., socializing with friends, watching television). When Gardner and Oswald (2007) compared 137 lottery winners (average winnings ~$200,000) to both non-winners and individuals who won smaller sums, the larger winners experienced greater mental stress that year, and a small improvement in psychological wellbeing after two years. Taken together these studies suggest that medium-sized windfalls may have a small impact toward improving wellbeing. Insight into the happiness of millionaires is limited to a single, sample from the 1983 Forbes list of wealthiest Americans (Diener, Horwitz, & Emmons, 1985). In this study, 49 wealthy individuals (each with a net worth over $125M) were compared to average earners from the same geographical areas. The very rich were, on average, somewhat happier than the average earners and reported moderately more satisfaction with life. The authors concluded that wealthier people are found to be happier than relatively poorer people, but the effects are small. However, this relative lack of data raises the question: does even more money bring even more happiness? In addition to the relationship between happiness and the sheer amount of wealth, we also investigate whether the source of that wealth predicts the happiness associated with it. Certainly, the manner in which people spend their money has been shown to influence happiness, with spending on experiences (Gilovich & Kumar, 2015; Van Boven & Gilovich, 2003) and spending on others and giving to charity (Dunn, Aknin, & Norton, 2008; 2014) typically associated with greater happiness than spending on material goods for the self. In addition, research has explored how the source of money affects subsequent spending of that money: framing money as a windfall versus an anticipated gain (Arkes et al., 1994), describing tax refunds as rebates versus bonuses (Epley & Gneezy, 2007), and making the source of a monetary gift as a relative versus an ill relative (Levav & McGraw, 2009) have all been shown to influence future spending. Building on this previous research, we explore whether the manner in which wealth is acquired – the source of wealth – is a predictor not of spending, but of happiness. Andrew Carnegie opined that a parent leaving their child "enormous wealth generally deadens the talents and energies of the child, leading to a less useful and less worthy life than they otherwise would" (Carnegie, 1962). Indeed, receiving a large inheritance significantly decreases people's labor force participation, offering some supporting evidence for this "Carnegie Conjecture" that inherited wealth leads to a decreased desire to work (Elinder, Erixson, & Ohlsson, 2012; Holtz-Eakin, Joulfaian, & Rosen, 1992). We explore whether Carnegie's words also apply to the well-being that people derive from their wealth – as a function of whether they earned or inherited it. Overview of the Studies We utilize data from two large samples of high-net-worth respondents. In Study 1, all respondents (N = 2,129, 70.4% male, median age = 45-54 years, sampled in 17 countries) reported a net worth of at least $1.5 million (median = $3-$7.9 million; Figure 1) and high incomes (median annual income = $100,000- $149,999; Respondents completed an item assessing their life satisfaction on a 7-point scale (Figure 3). In Study 2, all respondents (N = 2,026, 73.2% male, Mage = 54.5, SD = 12.8, sampled in 17 countries) reported a net worth of at least $1 million (median = $2-$4.9 million; Figure 4) and high incomes (median annual income = $100,000- $149,999; Figure 5). Respondents completed an item assessing their level of happiness with their lives in general on a 10-point scale (Figure 6). In both samples, net worth and income were converted to

US dollars, and respondents indicated the sources of their wealth, allowing us to calculate the percentage of earned wealth sources (e.g., from savings through earnings) and the percentage of unearned wealth sources (e.g., from an inheritance or marriage). Respondents and Design Ledbury Research conducted both surveys on behalf of a large financial institution in January 2012 and 2013 for commercial purposes; we use a subset of questions from the full survey instrument for our analyses. Per the stated guidance of the Harvard Business School Institutional Review Board for research using commercial data sets, we received approval for using data only after all respondent identifying information was removed. Study 1: Millionaires' Satisfaction with Life Materials and Procedure Respondents were high-net-worth individuals (N = 2,129) sampled in 17 countries in which the financial institution operates: 24.1% in the United States, 24.4% in the United Kingdom, and 79.2% in developed countries. Respondents were primarily male (70.4%) and middle aged (median age group = 45-54 years old). All respondents reported a net worth of at least $1.5 million (median net worth = $3-$7.9 million), and high incomes (median annual income = $100,000- $149,999). Respondents first rated their current net worth, defined as the total value of their savings, investments and assets minus any borrowing/mortgages (percentage endorsing each option in parentheses): (a) under $375,000, (b) $375,000 - $749,999, (c) $750,000 - $999,999, (d) $1 million - $1.49 million, (e) $1.5 million - $2.9 million (48.6%), (f) $3 million - $7.9 million (28.2%), (g) $8 million - $14.9 million (11.6%), (h) 15 million + (11.6%), (i) would rather not say. Respondents who indicated a net worth of under $1.5 million or who responded (i) were screened out of the survey (a decision made by the survey organization prior to data collection). Respondents then completed a series of questions included by the sponsoring organization. Finally, respondents rated their satisfaction with their life in general: "All things considered, I am satisfied with my life" on a 1 (Strongly Disagree) to 7 (Strongly Agree) scale. Such single-item measures assessing life satisfaction are commonly used in both panel data (e.g., Blanchflower & Oswald, 2004; Lucas & Donnellan, 2012) and convenience samples (e.g., Diener, Horwitz & Emmons, 1985; Dunn et al., 2008) and have been found to be highly reliable (Abdel-Khalek, 2006). Respondents reported their individual income on an annual basis, including any bonuses and/or investment income (percentage endorsing each option in parentheses): (a) no current income (1.2%), (b) under $50,000 (34.6%), (c) $50,000 - $99,000 (10.4%), (d) $100,000 - $149,999 (9.1%), (e)

$150,000 - $199,999 (6.2%), (f) $200,000 - $249,999 (5.0%), (g) $250,000 - $499,999 (9.6%), (h) $500,000 - $999,999 (17.1%), (i) 1 million + (3.4%), (j) prefer not to answer (3.4%). The few respondents (n=25) who chose (a) were grouped with those who chose (b) in the "under $50,000" category; those who endorsed (j) were excluded from all analyses of income (n = 72). All respondents were then asked, "Which of the following have contributed the most to your overall wealth?" with the following response options (percentage endorsing each option in parentheses): (a) inheritance (24.8%), (b) spouse/partner (12.5%), (c) savings through earnings/bonuses over time (49.1%), (d) profits/assets from business(es) (38.1%), (e) large bonus (28.9%), (g) personal investments (51.7%), (h) profit from property (36.8%), (i) other (6.2%). Respondents could report multiple sources of wealth. We summed the total number of sources for each respondent, and the number of instances listed that wealth was inherited or the result of a spouse/marriage for each respondent; we divided these instances by the total number of sources to create a "percent of unearned wealth sources" variable. To categorize these sources of wealth, we asked a sample of 100 participants from Amazon's Mechanical Turk (Mage = 38.87, SD = 12.46; 50.0% female, 85.0% Caucasian) to rate all sources of wealth on the extent they considered each to be earned on a 7-point scale (ranging from 1, definitely not earned, to 7, definitely earned). Participants rated the inheritance and spouse/partner sources as unearned (as demonstrated by mean ratings significantly lower than the midpoint of the 7-point scale; all $ps < .05$), and all other sources as being earned (with mean ratings significantly higher than the scale midpoint; all $ps < .001$). Net worth and personal income data were assessed in banded groups; we therefore created banded dummies for these variables in our analyses (see Table 1 for means, standard deviations and correlations among all study variables). In Step 1 of a four-step hierarchical regression (Table 2), we included only net worth dummy variables as predictors of life satisfaction, using respondents who reported a net worth of $1.5-2.9M – the modal response – as the reference group (Field, 2009). In Step 2 we included demographic variables previously shown to predict life satisfaction (e.g., Kahneman & Deaton, 2010; Di Tella & MacCulloch, 2008; Vendrik, 2013): gender, age, a polynomial term for age, marital status, and being retired. In Step 3, we include respondents' country of residence variables, and coded dummy variables using United States as the reference group. In Step 4, we included the "percent of unearned wealth sources" measure of respondents' reports of the sources of their wealth. Compared to respondents with a net worth of $1.5-2.9M, respondents with a net worth of $3-7.9M were not more satisfied with life ($ß = -.01$; $p = .62$, $d = .02$); those with a net worth of $8-14.9M were significantly more satisfied ($ß = .06$, $p = .004$, $d = .15$), and those with a net worth of $15M+ were marginally more satisfied ($ß = .04$, $p = .09$, $d = .10$). However, as Table 3 shows, these differences were small in absolute magnitude, with scores on a 7-point scale ranging from 5.79 to 5.97. These effects are consistent with, but relatively smaller than, effects observed for nationally representative samples at lower levels of wealth and income – where beta ranges from .06 to .40 (e.g., Blanchflower & Oswald, 2004; Clark & Oswald, 2002; Deaton, 2008; Diener, Sandvik, Seidlitz & Diener, 1993; Di Tella & MacCulloch, 2008; Di Tella, Haisken-De New & MacCulloch, 2010; Di Tella, MacCulloch & Oswald, 2003; Hagerty, 2000; Kahneman & Deaton, 2010; Stevenson & Wolfers, 2008; Vendrik, 2013) – perhaps demonstrating the marginal utility of wealth on well-being. In addition, the percentage of wealth sources that was unearned was negatively related to life satisfaction ($ß = -.05$, $p = .02$, $d = .10$), suggesting that earning rather than inheriting wealth is associated with greater happiness. However, as Table 4 shows, these differences were small in absolute magnitude, with scores on a 7-point scale ranging from 5.22 to 6.02. Life satisfaction was also predicted by gender (males were happier than females) and being married ($ps < .01$). We next evaluated personal income as a predictor of happiness. We used the modal income group – respondents making < $50K – as the reference group (Table 5), conducting the same 4-step regression as above but including banded income dummies in addition to banded wealth dummies. The pattern of results was unchanged for wealth when we included income. The only income group that differed from the < $50K reference group were respondents with $1M+ in income, though these respondents reported lower levels of satisfaction ($ß = -.05$; $p = .03$, $d = .18$). Study 2: Millionaires' Happiness To replicate our two primary findings from Study 1 – that very high levels of wealth are associated with significantly – though moderately – greater happiness, and that earned wealth is associated with greater happiness than inherited wealth, our second sample also included high net worth individuals recruited by Ledbury Research, using a similar survey with some small changes. First, well-being was assessed by general ratings of happiness: Respondents rated their current level of happiness with their lives in general, a measure used in previous research and correlates with measures of life satisfaction and demonstrates similar predictive ability (Di Tella & MacCulloch, 2008; Di Tella, Haisken-De New & MacCulloch, 2010; Howell & Howell, 2008; Kahneman, Krueger, Schkade, Schwarz, & Stone, 2004). Second, the survey organization included all participants with a net worth of over $1M (as opposed to $1.5M in Study 1), and assessed wealth in four slightly narrower banded groups. Third, household income was assessed rather than individual income; household income is a reliable predictor of wellbeing (Howell & Howell, 2008). Finally, following previous research assessing the accuracy of people's predictions about the relationship between assets and happiness (Aknin et al., 2009; Cone & Gilovich, 2010; Kahneman, Krueger, Schkade, Schwarz, & Stone, 2006), we assess millionaires' beliefs about the impact of more wealth on their happiness. Materials and Procedure Respondents were high-net-worth individuals (N = 2,026) sampled in 17 countries in which the financial institution operates: 25.5% in the United States, 24.7% in the United Kingdom, and 67.7% in developed countries. Respondents were primarily male (73.2%) and middle aged (Mage = 54.5, SD = 12.8). All respondents reported a net worth of at least $1 million (median net worth = $2-$4.9 million), and high incomes (median annual income = $100,000- $149,999). Ledbury Research recruits high net worth individuals from a large global panel, making it unlikely that the same respondents completed both surveys; because data are deidentified, we cannot link the two data sets to crosscheck. Respondents first rated their current net worth, defined as the total value of their savings, investments and assets minus any borrowing/ mortgages (percentage endorsing each option in parentheses): (a) under $250,000, (b) $250,000 - $499,999, (c) $500,000 - $749,999, (d) $750,000 - $999,999, (e) $1 million - $1.9 million (49.0%), (f) $2 million - $4.9 million (32.4%), (g) $5 million - $9.9 million (8.7%), (h) $10 million + (9.9%), (i) would rather not say. Respondents who indicated a net worth of under $1 million or who responded (i) were screened out of the survey (a decision made by the survey organization prior to data collection). Respondents then completed a series of questions included by the sponsoring organization. Finally, respondents rated their general happiness: "How would you rate your current level of happiness with your life in general on a 1 to 10 scale, where 1 equals 'Extremely Unhappy' and 10 equals 'Extremely Happy'?" Respondents who did not answer "10" to the happiness question were then asked, "What increase in your wealth do you think would move you one point higher on the scale?" and given six options: (a) no increase would change my happiness, (b) a 10% increase in your current wealth,

(c) a 50% increase in your current wealth, (d) double your current wealth, (e) 5 times your current wealth, and (f) 10 times your current wealth. Only respondents who had not answered "no increase would change my happiness" to the 1-point increase question and had not reported a "9" or "10" to the happiness question, then answered "What increase in your wealth do you think would move you to a 10 on the scale (extremely happy)?" using the same six response options. Respondents reported their household income on an annual basis, including any bonuses and/or investment income (percentage endorsing each option in parentheses): (a) no current income (0.2%), (b) under $50,000 (3.8%), (c) $50,000 - $99,999 (21.6%), (d) $100,000 - $149,999 (22.0%), (e) $150,000 - $199,999 (11.9%), (f) $200,000 - $249,999 (8.7%), (g) $250,000 - $499,999 (13.2%), (h) $500,000 - $999,999 (5.1%), (i) 1 million + (6.7%), (j) prefer not to answer (6.8%). The few respondents (n=4) who chose (a) were grouped with those who chose (b) in the "under $50,000" category; those who endorsed (j) were excluded from all analyses of income (n = 138). All respondents were then asked, "Which of the following have contributed the most to your overall wealth?" with the following response options (percentage endorsing each option in parentheses): (a) inheritance (25.4%), (b) spouse/partner (18.4%), (c) savings through earnings/ bonuses over time (55.5%), (d) profits/assets from business(es) (32.9%), (e) profits/assets from business(es) (15.5%), (f) large bonus (12.9%), (g) personal investments (55.2%), (h) profit from property (33.6%), (i) other (1.1%). Respondents could report multiple sources of wealth. We summed the total number of sources for each respondent, and the number of instances listed that wealth was inherited or the result of a spouse/marriage for each respondent; we divided these instances by the total number of sources to create a "percent of unearned wealth sources" variable. Results Net worth and household income data were assessed in banded groups, albeit in different bands than the previous sample; we again created banded dummies for these variables in our analyses (see Table 6 for means, standard deviations and correlations among all study variables). We used the same four-step hierarchical regression as Study 1 (Table 7), including the same variables as before in each step. Compared to respondents with a net worth of $1-1.9M, respondents with a net worth of either $2-4.9M or $5-9.9M were not happier (ßs = .01 and -.02, ps = .57 and .40, ds = .02 and .06); those with a net worth of $10M+, however, were significantly happier The Happiness of Millionaires (ß = .06, p = .02, d = .16). However, as Table 8 shows, these differences were again small in absolute magnitude, with scores on a 10-point scale ranging from 7.72 to 8.03. As in Sample 1, these effects were also consistent with, but relatively smaller than, effects observed in nationally representative samples at lower levels of wealth and income. Also as in Sample 1, the percentage of wealth that was unearned was negatively related to happiness ($ß = -.05$, $p = .04$, $d = .09$). However, as Table 9 shows, these differences were again small in absolute magnitude, with scores on a 10-point scale ranging from 7.38 to 8.05. Happiness was also significantly predicted by being married, and being retired ($ps < .007$). Predictions of the amount of wealth needed to increase happiness were similar across wealth levels. The most common response for a 1-point increase in happiness was "no increase" (36.8%), followed by "100% more" (22.3%), and "50% more" (18.4%); this pattern did not differ by wealth, $\chi2$ $(15) = 7.43$, $p = .95$, $d = .01$ (see Table 10). The percentage increase needed was larger for an increase in happiness to a "perfect 10," with "1,000% more" the most frequent (26.8%) followed by "500% more" (24.5%), and "100% more" (23.2%); this pattern again did not differ by wealth, $\chi2$ (15) $= 16.62$, $p = .34$, $d = .04$ (see Table 11). We note that "no increase would change my happiness" item is ambiguous, such that endorsing this item could either indicate that respondents were happy with the wealth they had (such that no change would affect their happiness), or that the level of wealth needed to change their happiness was unrealistically large (such that no increase exists that would affect their happiness). Despite this ambiguity, we note that for both questions, the majority of respondents reported a specific numerical change in wealth that they believed would change their happiness.We evaluated household income as a predictor of happiness, including all banded net worth and banded income variables in the same regression (Table 12), which did not change the pattern of results for net worth: again, only respondents worth $10M+ were significantly happier than those worth $1-1.9M ($ß = .05$, $p = .04$, $d = .13$). No income groups differed from the < $50K reference group. Thus while both samples show converging evidence that high levels of wealth are associated with greater happiness, results for income are more mixed, with higher incomes in Study 1 negatively associated with life satisfaction but in Study 2 not associated with happiness. While we can only speculate, Study 1 assessed personal income and Study 2 household income, and these two metrics may relate to different aspects of well-being. Discussion Is greater wealth associated with greater well-being? Overall, using two large samples of millionaires with two measures of well-being (happiness in general and life satisfaction), we find consistent evidence that somewhat higher levels of wealth are not associated with higher well-being, but substantially higher levels (greater than $8M in Sample 1, greater than $10M in Sample 2) are linked to modestly greater well-being. Augmenting some models of the money-happiness link that suggest a "flattening out" of the curve once an income threshold has been reached – for example, $75,000 (Kahneman & Deaton, 2010) – our results suggest that the curve does not fully flatten out: great wealth does predict greater happiness. Research suggests that wealth can have mixed effects on happiness: while the wealthy are more likely to engage in some behaviors associated with increased well-being – such as volunteering at non-profit organizations (Dury et al., 2015; Tang et al., 2008), giving money to those in need (Smeets, Bauer, & Gneezy, 2015), and donating their used items for reuse (Granzin & Olsen, 1991) – they are less likely to engage in other behaviors linked to well-being – such as behaving charitably toward others (Piff, Kraus, Cote, Cheng, & Keltner, 2010). Our results suggest that despite these conflicting effects of wealth on the pursuit of happiness-inducing activities, sufficiently high wealth does indeed predict modestly greater happiness. Why might greater wealth lead to greater happiness among millionaires? Diener, Horwitz and Emmon's (1985) study of millionaires shows that the wealthy believe that money increases their happiness when used to help others and the world, and that money provides increased freedom to choose leisure activities and friends. Indeed, wealth enables people to take greater control of their lives, by giving the wealthy greater autonomy over how they choose to spend their time (Gallo & Matthews, 2003; Kraus, Piff, Mendoza-Denton, Rheinschmidt, & Keltner, 2012), and such feelings have been associated with higher life satisfaction (Howell & Howell, 2008). While a number of researchers have cited need theory to explain the diminishing marginal effect of wealth and well-being (e.g., Howell & Howell, 2008), perhaps at the higher end, wealth increases millionaires' sense of efficacy in carrying out goals (Lachman & Weaver, 1998). In addition, it is possible that wealth helps millionaires' to achieve the fundamental human goal of high status (Anderson, Hildreth, & Howland, 2015). While our datasets do not allow us to examine these potential mediating processes, we hope that future research explores these issues in more depth. In addition, both samples document a novel factor determining the wealthhappiness link: whether millionaires earned or inherited their wealth. While previous research has focused on the effect of spending money in different ways (Dunn et al., 2014; Gilovich & Kumar, 2015), we focus instead on the effects on well-being of the manner in which money was acquired. Whereas previous research demonstrates that inheriting wealth can decrease desire for employment, we show that inheriting wealth has a psychological effect as well: the percentage of wealth that people earned serves as a positive predictor of general happiness. While we found the percentage of unearned wealth sources to negatively predict happiness, our data does not allow us to calculate the actual proportion of wealth that was earned or unearned. While a convenience sample evaluated receiving an inheritance and acquiring money through marriage as an unearned source of wealth, we cannot be certain that recipients of inheritances and wealth through marriage would evaluate these sources of wealth as being unearned. Future research should evaluate how perceptions of earning wealth impact well-being; one possibility is that the effort of earning leads people to value their wealth more, in the same way that effort leads people to more highly value social groups, consumer products, and even psychotherapy (Aronson & Mills, 1959; Axsom & Cooper, 1965; Norton, Mochon, & Ariely, 2012). In sum, we show that, in addition to microeconomic factors that determine the relationship between money and happiness – such as economic inequality (Oishi, Kesebir, & Diener, 2011) – a novel microeconomic factor shapes happiness: whether wealth was inherited or earned. We note that, as in all cross-sectional data assessing the money-happiness link, our results are correlational: we can say neither that very high levels of wealth cause greater happiness, nor that earning wealth causes greater happiness than inheriting it. For example, causation may run in the opposite direction, with higher well-being leading to higher wealth (Lyubomirsky, King, & Diener, 2005); indeed, happier people are more likely to obtain a college degree, to get promoted in their jobs, and to earn greater wealth (De Neve & Oswald, 2012). We are also unable to assess whether inheritors and earners differ on other variables such as intelligence or conscientiousness, which may account for the differences in happiness we observe; for instance, our effects may vary as a function of the extent to which millionaires measure their self-worth on their financial success (Park, Ward, & Naragon-Gainey, 2017). In addition, because the two samples assessed wealth using different banded groups, we are unable to identify a common "tipping point" in which happiness should be greatest, though the two samples do suggest that this tipping point occurs only at high levels of wealth compared to lower levels of wealth. And finally, while the sample sizes of our study are relatively large for this population – millionaires – we cannot be certain that they are representative of millionaires in general (though of course, millionaires are by definition an unrepresentative group). Still, taken together, these results suggest that millionaires' belief that increased wealth is associated with increased happiness is more likely to be realized at high levels of wealth, and when they have earned it.

CHAPTER EIGHT

Rich people are committed to being rich. Poor people want to be rich.

Ask most people if they want to be rich and they'd look at you as if you were crazy. "Of course I want to be rich," they'd say. The truth, however, is that most people don't really want to be rich. Why? Because they have a lot of negative wealth files in their subconscious mind that tell them there is something wrong with being rich. At our Millionaire Mind Intensive Seminar, one of the questions we ask people is "What are some of the possible negatives about being rich or trying to get rich?" Here's what some people have to say. See if you can relate to any of these. "What if I make it and lose it? Then I'll really be a failure." "I'll never know if people like me for myself or for my money." "I'll be at the highest tax bracket and have to give half my money to the government." "It's too much work." "I could lose my health trying." "My friends and family will say, 'Who do you think you are?' and criticize me." "Everyone's going to want a handout." "I could be robbed." "My kids could be kidnapped." "It's too much responsibility. I'll have to manage all that money. I'll have to really understand investments. I'll have to worry about tax strategies and asset protection and have to hire expensive accountants and lawyers. Yuck, what a hassle." And on and on it goes.... As I mentioned earlier, each of us has a wealth file inside the cabinet called our mind. This file contains our personal beliefs that include why being rich would be wonderful. However, for many people, this file also includes information as to why being rich might not be so wonderful. This means they have mixed internal messages about wealth. One part of them gleefully says, "Having more money will make life a lot more fun." But then another part screams, "Yeah, but I'm going to have to work like a dog! What fun is that?" One part says, "I'll be able to travel the world." Then the other part chirps in, "Yeah, and everyone in the world will want a handout." These mixed messages may seem innocent enough, but in reality, they are one of the major reasons most people never become rich. You can look at it like this. The universe, which is another way of saying "higher power," is akin to a big mail-order department. It is constantly delivering people, events, and things to you. You "order" what you get by sending energetic messages out to the universe based on your predominant beliefs. Again, based on the Law of Attraction, the universe will do its best to say yes and support you. But if you have mixed messages in your file, the universe can't understand what you want.

RICH PEOPLE ARE COMMITTED TO BEING RICH

One minute the universe hears that you want to be rich, so it begins sending you opportunities for wealth. But then it hears you say, "Rich people are greedy," so the universe begins to support you in not having much money. But then you think, "Having a lot of money makes life so much more enjoyable," so the poor universe, dazed and confused, restarts sending you opportunities for more money. The next day you're in an uninspired mood so you think, "Money's not that important." The frustrated universe finally screams, "Make up your frickin' mind! I'll get you what you want, just tell me what it is!" The number one reason most people don't get what they want is that they don't know what they want. Rich people are totally clear that they want wealth. They are unwavering in their desire. They are fully committed to creating wealth. As long as it's legal, moral, and ethical, they will do whatever it takes to have wealth. Rich people do not send mixed messages to the universe. Poor people do. Poor people have plenty of good reasons as to why getting and actually being rich might be a problem. Consequently, they are not 100 percent certain they really want to be rich. Their message to the universe is confusing. Their message to others is confusing. And why does all of this confusion happen? Because their message to themselves is confusing. Earlier we talked about the power of intention. I know it might be hard to believe, but you always get what you want— what you subconsciously want, not what you say you want. You might emphatically deny this and respond, "That's crazy! Why would I want to struggle?" And my question for you is exactly the same: "I don't know. Why would you want to struggle?" If you want to discover the reason, I invite you to attend the Millionaire Mind Intensive Seminar, where you will identify your money blueprint. The answer will be staring you in the face. Put bluntly, if you are not achieving the wealth you say you desire, there's a good chance it's because, first, you subconsciously don't really want wealth, or second, you're not willing to do what it takes to create it. Let's explore this further. There are actually three levels of so-called wanting. The first level is "I want to be rich." That's another way of saying, "I'll take it if it falls in my lap." Wanting alone is useless. Have you noticed that wanting doesn't necessarily lead to "having"? Notice also that wanting without having leads to more wanting. Wanting becomes habitual and leads only to itself, creating a perfect circle that goes exactly nowhere. Wealth does not come from merely wanting it. How do you know this is true? With a simple reality check: billions of people want to be rich, relatively few are. The second level of wanting is "I choose to be rich." This entails deciding to become rich. Choosing is a much stronger energy and goes hand in hand with being responsible for creating your reality. The word decision comes from the Latin word decidere, which means "to kill off any other alternatives." Choosing is better but not best. The third level of wanting is "I commit to being rich." The definition of the word commit is "to devote oneself unreservedly." This means holding absolutely nothing back; giving 100 percent of everything you've got to achieving wealth. It means being willing to do whatever it takes for as long as it takes. This is the warrior's way. No excuses, no ifs, no buts, no maybes—and failure is not an option. The warrior's way is simple: "I will be rich or I will die trying." "I commit to being rich." Try saying that to yourself.... What comes up for you? For some, it feels empowering. For others, it feels daunting. Most people would never truly commit to being rich. If you asked them, "Would you bet your life that in the next ten years you will be wealthy?" most would say, "No way!" That's the difference between rich people and poor people. It's precisely because people won't truly commit to being rich that they are not rich and most likely never will be. Some might say, "Harv, what are you talking about? I work my butt off, I'm trying real hard. Of course I'm committed to being rich." And I would reply, "That you're trying means little. The definition of commitment is to devote oneself unreservedly." The key word is unreservedly. Which means you're putting everything, and I mean everything, you've got into it. Most people I know who are not financially successful have limits on how much they are willing to do, how much they are willing to risk, and how much they are willing to sacrifice. Although they think they're willing to do whatever it takes, upon deeper questioning I always find they have plenty of conditions around what they are willing to do and not do to succeed! I hate to have to be the one to tell you this, but getting rich is not a stroll in the park, and anyone who tells you it is either knows a heck of a lot more than me or is a little out of integrity. In my experience, getting rich takes focus, courage, knowledge, expertise, 100 percent of your effort, a never-giveup attitude, and of course a rich mind-set. You also have to believe in your heart of hearts that you can create wealth and that you absolutely deserve it. Again, what this means is that, if you are not fully, totally, and truly committed to creating wealth, chances are you won't.

Rich people believe: "I create my life."	Poor people believe: "Life happens to me."

Wealth Principle:	When you are complaining, you become a living, breathing "crap magnet."

Are you willing to work sixteen hours a day? Rich people are. Are you willing to work seven days a week and give up most of your weekends? Rich people are. Are you willing to sacrifice seeing your family, your friends, and give up your recreations and hobbies? Rich people are. Are you willing to risk all your time, energy, and start-up capital with no guarantee of returns? Rich people are. For a time, hopefully a short time but often a long time, rich people are ready and willing to do all of the above. Are you? Maybe you'll be lucky and you won't have to work long or hard or sacrifice anything. You can wish for that, but I sure wouldn't count on it. Again, rich people are committed enough to do whatever it takes. Period. It's interesting to note, however, that once you do commit, the universe will bend over backward to support you. One of my favorite passages is by explorer W. H. Murray, who wrote the following during one of the first Himalayan expeditions: Until one is committed, there is hesitancy, the chance to draw back, always ineffectiveness. Concerning all acts of initiative (and creation), there is one elementary truth, the ignorance of which kills countless ideas and splendid plans: that the moment one definitely commits oneself, then providence moves too. A whole stream of events issues from the decision, raising in one's favor all manner of unforeseen incidents, meetings, and material assistance, which no man could have dreamt would have come his way. In other words, the universe will assist you, guide you, support you, and even create miracles for you. But first, you have to commit!

Place your hand on your heart and say... "I commit to being rich." Touch your head and say... "I have a millionaire mind!" MILLIONAIRE MIND ACTIONS 1. Write a short paragraph on exactly why creating wealth is important to you. Be specific. 2. Meet with a friend or family member who is willing to support you. Tell that person you want to evoke the power of commitment for the purpose of creating greater success. Put your hand on your heart, look that person in the eye, and repeat the following statement: "I, _____ [your name], do hereby commit to becoming a millionaire or more by _____ [date]." Tell your partner to say, "I believe in you." Then you say, "Thank you." P.S. To strengthen your commitment, I invite you to commit directly to me at www.millionairemindbook .com, then print out your commitment and post it on your wall.

The Law of Income: You will be paid in direct proportion to the value you deliver according to the marketplace. The key word is value. It's important to know that four factors determine your value in the marketplace: supply, demand, quality, and quantity. In my experience, the factor that presents the biggest challenge for most people is the quantity. The quantity factor simply means, how much of your value do you actually deliver to the marketplace? Another way of stating this is, how many people do you actually serve or affect? In my business, for instance, some trainers prefer teaching small groups of twenty people at a time, others are comfortable with a hundred participants in the room, others like an audience of five hundred, and still others love audiences of a thousand to five thousand or more. Is there a difference in income among these trainers? You better believe there is! Consider the network marketing business. Is there a difference in income between someone who has ten people in his or her down-line and someone who has ten thousand people? I would think so! Near the beginning of this book, I mentioned that I owned a chain of retail fitness stores. From the moment I even considered going into this business, my intention was to have one hundred successful stores and affect tens of thousands of people. My competitor, on the other hand, who started six months after me, had the intention of owning one successful store. In the end, she earned a decent living. I got rich! How do you want to live your life? How do you want to play the game? Do you want to play in the big leagues or in the little leagues, in the majors or the minors? Are you going to play big or play small? It's your choice. Most people choose to play small. Why? First, because of fear. They're scared to death of failure and they're even more frightened of success. Second, people play small because they feel small. They feel unworthy. They don't feel they're good enough or important enough to make a real difference in people's lives. But hear this: Your life is not just about you. It's also about contributing to others. It's about living true to your mission and reason for being here on this earth at this time. It's about adding your piece of the puzzle to the world. Most people are so stuck in their egos that everything revolves around me, me, and more me. But if you want to be rich in the truest sense of the word, it can't only be about you. It has to include adding value to other people's lives.

One of the greatest inventors and philosophers of our time, Buckminster Fuller, said, "The purpose of our lives is to add value to the people of this generation and those that follow." We each came to this earth with natural talents, things we're just naturally good at. These gifts were given to you for a reason: to use and share with others. Research shows that the happiest people are those who use their natural talents to the utmost. Part of your mission in life then must be to share your gifts and value with as many people as possible. That means being willing to play big. Do you know the definition of an entrepreneur? The definition we use in our programs is "a person who solves problems for people at a profit." That's right, an entrepreneur is nothing more than a "problem solver." So I ask you, would you rather solve problems for more people or fewer people? If you replied more, then you need to start thinking bigger and decide to help massive numbers of people—thousands, even millions. The by-product is that the more people you help, the "richer" you become, mentally, emotionally, spiritually, and definitely financially. Make no mistake, every person on this planet has a mission. If you are living right now, there's a reason for it. Richard Bach, in his book Jonathan Livingston Seagull, is asked, "How will I know when I've completed my mission?" The answer? "If you are still breathing, you are not done." What I have witnessed is too many people not doing their job, not fulfilling their duty, or dharma as it's called in Sanskrit. I watch too many people playing far too small, and too many people allowing their fear-based ego selves to rule them. The result is that too many of us are not living up to our full potential, in terms of both our own lives and our contribution to others. It comes down to this: If not you, then who? Again, everyone has his or her unique purpose. Maybe you're a real estate investor and buy properties to rent them out and make money on cash flow and appreciation. What's your mission? How do you help? There's a good chance you add value to your community by helping families find affordable housing they may not otherwise be able to find. Now the question is how many families and people can you assist? Are you willing to help ten instead of one, twenty instead of ten, one hundred instead of twenty? This is what I mean by playing big. In her wonderful book A Return to Love, author Marianne Williamson puts it this way: You are a child of God. Your playing small does not serve the world. There is nothing enlightened about shrinking so that other people won't feel insecure around you. We are all meant to shine, as children do. We were born to make manifest the glory of God that is within us. It is not just in some of us; it is in everyone. And as we let our own light shine, we unconsciously give other people permission to do the same. As we are liberated from our own fear, our presence automatically liberates others. The world doesn't need more people playing small. It's time to stop hiding out and start stepping out. It's time to stop needing and start leading. It's time to start sharing your gifts instead of hoarding them or pretending they don't exist. It's time you started playing the game of life in a "big" way. In the end, small thinking and small actions lead to being both broke and unfulfilled. Big thinking and big actions.

lead to having both money and meaning. The choice is yours! DECLARATION: Place your hand on your heart and say... "I think big! I choose to help thousands and thousands of people!"

Rich people see opportunities. Poor people see obstacles. Rich people see potential growth. Poor people see potential loss. Rich people focus on the rewards. Poor focus on the risks. It comes down to the age-old question, "Is the glass half empty or half full?" We're not talking positive thinking here, we're talking about your habitual perspective on the world. Poor people make choices based upon fear. Their minds are constantly scanning for what is wrong or could go wrong in any situation. Their primary mind-set is "What if it doesn't work?" or, more often, "It won't work." Middle-class people are slightly more optimistic. Their mind-set is "I sure hope this works." Rich people, as we've said earlier, take responsibility for the results in their lives and act upon the mind-set "It will work because I'll make it work." Rich people expect to succeed. They have confidence in their abilities, they have confidence in their creativity, and they believe that should the doo-doo hit the fan, they can find another way to succeed.

Generally speaking, the higher the reward, the higher the risk. Because they constantly see opportunity, rich people are willing to take a risk. Rich people believe that, if worse comes to worst, they can always make their money back. Poor people, on the other hand, expect to fail. They lack confidence in themselves and in their abilities. Poor people believe that should things not work out, it would be catastrophic. And because they constantly see obstacles, they are usually unwilling to take a risk. No risk, no reward. For the record, being willing to risk doesn't necessarily mean that you are willing to lose. Rich people take educated risks. This means that they research, do their due diligence, and make decisions based on solid information and facts. Do rich people take forever to get educated? No. They do what they can in as short a time as possible, then make an informed decision to go for it or not. Although poor people claim to be preparing for an opportunity, what they're usually doing is stalling. They're scared to death, hemming and hawing for weeks, months, and even years on end, and by then the opportunity usually disappears. Then they rationalize the situation by saying, "I was getting ready." Sure enough, but while they were "getting ready," the rich guy got in, got out, and made another fortune. I know what I'm about to say may sound a little strange considering how much I value self-responsibility. However, I do believe a certain element of what many people call luck is associated with getting rich, or, for that matter, with being successful at anything. In football, it might be the opposing team's player fumbling on your own one-yard line with less than a minute to go, allowing your team to win the game. In golf it could be the errant shot that hits an out-of-bounds tree and bounces back onto the green, just three inches from the hole. In business, how many times have you heard of a guy who plops some money down on a piece of land in the boonies, and ten years later, some conglomerate decides it wants to build a shopping center or office building on it? This investor gets rich. So, was it a brilliant business move on his part or sheer luck? My guess is that it's a bit of both. The point, however, is that no luck—or anything else worthwhile—will come your way unless you take some form of action. To succeed financially, you have to do something, buy something, or start something. And when you do, is it luck or is it the universe or a higher power supporting you in its miraculous ways for having the courage and commitment to go for it? As far as I'm concerned, who cares what it is. It happens! Another key principle, pertinent here, is that rich people focus on what they want, while poor people focus on what they don't want.

Again, the universal law states, "What you focus on expands." Because rich people focus on the opportunities in everything, opportunities abound for them. Their biggest problem is handling all the incredible moneymaking possibilities they see. On the other hand, because poor people focus on the obstacles in everything, obstacles abound for them and their biggest problem is handling all the incredible obstacles they see. It's simple. Your field of focus determines what you find in life. Focus on opportunities and that's what you find. Focus on obstacles and that's what you find. I'm not saying that you don't take care of problems. Of course, handle problems as they arise, in the present. But keep your eye on your goal, keep moving toward your target. Put your time and energy into creating what you want. When obstacles arise, handle them, then quickly refocus on your vision. You do not make your life about solving problems. You don't spend all your time fighting fires. Those who do, move backward! You spend your time and energy in thought and deed, moving steadily forward, toward your goal. Do you want some simple but extremely rare advice? Here it is: If you want to get rich, focus on making, keeping, and investing your money. If you want to be poor, focus on spending your money. You can read a thousand books and take a hundred courses on success, but it all boils down to that. Remember, what you focus on expands. Rich people also understand that you can never know all the information beforehand. In another of our programs, Enlightened Warrior Training, we train people to access their inner power and succeed in spite of anything. In this course we teach a principle known as "Ready, fire, aim!" What do we mean? Get ready the best you can in as short a time as possible; take action; then correct along the way. It's nuts to think you can know everything that may happen in the future. It's delusional to believe you can prepare for every circumstance that might someday occur and pro- tect yourself from it. Did you know that there are no straight lines in the universe? Life doesn't travel in perfectly straight lines. It moves more like a winding river. More often than not, you can only see to the next bend, and only when you reach that next turn can you see more. The idea is to get in the game with whatever you've got, from wherever you are. I call this entering the corridor. For example, years ago I was planning on opening an all-night dessert café in Fort Lauderdale, Florida. I studied location options, the marketplace, and found out what equipment I'd need. I also researched the kinds of cakes, pies, ice creams, and coffees available. The first big problem—I got really fat! Eating my research wasn't helpful. So I asked myself, what would be the best way to study this business?" Then I heard this guy named Arvind, who was obviously a lot smarter than me, answer, "If you really want to learn a business, get into it. You don't have to own the darn thing from day one. Get in the corridor by getting a job in the arena. You'll learn more by sweeping up a restaurant and washing dishes than by ten years of research from the outside." (I told you he was a lot smarter than me.) And that's what I did. I got a job at Mother Butler's Pie Shop. I wish I could tell you that they immediately recognized my superb talents and started me as CEO. But alas, somehow they just didn't see, nor did they care about, my executive leadership skills, and so I began as a busboy. That's right, sweeping the floor and clearing dishes. Funny how the power of intention works, isn't it? You might think that I must really have had to swallow my pride to do this, but the truth is, I never looked at it that way. I was on a mission to learn the dessert business; I was grateful for the opportunity to learn it on someone else's "ticket" and make some pocket change to boot. During my tenure as the pie busboy, I spent as much time as possible shootin' the doo-doo with the manager about revenues and profits, checking boxes to find out the names of the suppliers, and helping the baker at 4:00 a.m., to learn about equipment, ingredients, and problems that could occur. A full week went by and I guess I was pretty good at my job, because the manager sat me down, fed me some pie (yuck!), and promoted me to...(drumroll please) cashier ! I thought about it long and hard, for exactly a nanosecond, and replied, "Thanks but no thanks." First, there was no way I could learn much being stuck behind a cash register. Second, I'd already learned what I came to learn. Mission accomplished! So that's what I mean by being in the "corridor." It means entering the arena where you want to be in the future, in any capacity, to get started. This is far and away the best way to learn about a business, because you see it from the inside. Second, you can make the contacts you need, which you could never have made from the outside. Third, once you're in the corridor, many other doors of opportunity may open to you. That is, once you witness what's really going on, you may discover a niche for yourself that you hadn't recognized before. Fourth, you may find that you don't really like this field, and thank goodness you found out before you got in too deep!

Successful people look at other successful people as a means to motivate themselves. They see other successful people as models to learn from. They say to themselves, "If they can do it, I can do it." As I mentioned earlier, modeling is one of the primary ways that people learn. Rich people are grateful that others have succeeded before them so that they now have a blueprint to follow that will make it easier to attain their own success. Why reinvent the wheel? There are proven methods for success that work for virtually everyone who applies them. Consequently, the fastest and easiest way to create wealth is to learn exactly how rich people, who are masters of money, play the game. The goal is to simply model their inner and outer strategies. It just makes sense: if you take the exact same actions and have the exact same mind-set, chances are good you will get the exact same results. That's what I did and that's what this entire book is about. Contrary to the rich, when poor people hear about other people's success, they often judge them, criticize them, mock them, and try to pull them down to their own level. How many of you know people like this? How many of you know family members like this? The question is, how can you possibly learn from or be inspired by someone you put down? Whenever I'm introduced to an extremely rich person, I create a way to get together with them. I want to talk to them, learn how they think, exchange contacts, and if we have other things in common, possibly become personal friends with them. By the way, if you think I'm wrong for preferring to be friends with rich people, perhaps you'd rather I pick friends who are broke? I don't think so! As I've mentioned before, energy is contagious, and I have no interest in subjecting myself to theirs! I was recently doing a radio interview and a woman called in with an excellent question: "What do I do if I'm positive and want to grow, but my husband is a downer? Do I leave him? Do I try and get him to change? What?" I hear this question at least a hundred times a week when I'm teaching our courses. Almost everyone asks the same question: "What if the people I'm closest to aren't into personal growth and even put me down for it?" Here's the answer I gave the woman on the call, what I tell people at our courses, and what I'm suggesting to you. First, don't bother trying to get negative people to change or come to the course. That's not your job. Your job is to use what you've learned to better yourself and your life. Be the model, be successful, be happy, then maybe—and I stress maybe—they'll see the light (in you) and want some of it. Again, energy is contagious. Darkness dissipates in light. People actually have to work hard to stay "dark" when light is all around them. Your job is simply to be the best you can be. If they choose to ask you your secret, tell them. Second, keep in mind another principle that we feature in our Wizard Training, which is a course about manifesting what you want while staying calm, centered, and peaceful. It states, "Everything happens for a reason and that reason is there to assist me." Yes, it's much more difficult to be posi- tive and conscious around people and circumstances that are negative, but that's your test! Just as steel is hardened in the fire, if you can remain true to your values while others around you are full of doubt and even condemnation, you'll grow faster and stronger. Also remember that "nothing has meaning except for the meaning we give it." Recall in Part I of this book, we discussed how we usually end up identifying with or rebelling against one or both of our parents, depending on how we "framed" their actions. From now on, I want you to practice reframing other people's negativity as a reminder of how not to be. The more negative they are, the more reminders you have about how ugly that way of being really is. I'm not suggesting you tell them this. Just do it, without condemning them for how they are. For if you do begin to judge, criticize, and put them down for who they are and what they do, then you are no better than them. Worse comes to worst, if you just can't handle their nonsupportive energy anymore, if it's bringing you down to a point where you're not able to grow, you may have to make some courageous decisions about who you are and how you want to live the rest of your life. I'm not suggesting you do anything rash, but I for one would never live with a person who was negative and pooh-poohed my desire to learn and grow, be it personally, spiritually, or financially. I wouldn't do that to myself because I respect myself and my life and I deserve to be as happy and successful as possible. The way I figure it, there are over 6.3 billion people in the world and there's no way I'm going to saddle myself with a downer. Either they move up or I move on! Again, energy is contagious: either you affect people or infect people. The same holds true the opposite way around; either people affect or infect you. Let me ask you a question: Would you hug and hold a person you knew had a severe case of the measles? Most people would say, "No way, I don't want to catch the measles." Well, I believe negative thinking is like having measles of the mind. Instead of itching, you get bitching; instead of scratching, you get bashing; instead of irritation, you get frustration. Now, do you really want to be close to people like that? I'm sure you've heard the saying "Birds of a feather flock together." Did you know that most people earn within 20 percent of the average income of their closest friends? That's why you'd better watch whom you associate with and choose whom you spend your time with carefully. From my experience, rich people don't just join the country club to play golf; they join to connect with other rich and successful people. There's another saying that goes "It's not what you know, it's who you know." As far as I'm concerned, you can take that to the bank. In short, "If you want to fly with the eagles, don't swim with the ducks!" I make it a point to only associate with successful, positive people, and just as importantly, I disassociate from negative ones. I also make it a point to remove myself from toxic situations. I see no reason for infecting myself with poisonous energy. Among these I would include arguing, gossiping, and backstabbing. I would also include watching "mindless" television, unless you use it specifically as a relaxation strategy instead of your sole form of entertainment. When I watch TV, it's usually sports. First, because I enjoy seeing masters at anything at work or in this case play, and second because I enjoy listening to the interviews after the games. I love listening to the mind-set of champions, and to me, anyone who has made it as far as the big leagues in any sport is a champion. Any athlete at that level has outcompeted tens of thousands of other players to get there at all, which makes each of them incredible to me. I love hearing their attitude when they win: "It was a great effort from the entire team. We did well but we still have improvements to make. It goes to show you that hard work pays off." I also love listening to their attitude when they lose: "It's only one game. We'll be back, we're just going to forget about this one and put our focus on the next game. We'll go back and talk about where we can do better, and then do whatever it takes to win." During the 2004 Olympic Games, Perdita Felicien, a Canadian and the reigning world champion in the hundredmeter hurdles, was heavily favored to win the gold medal. In the final race, she hit the first hurdle and fell hard. She wasn't able to complete the race. Extremely upset, she had tears in her eyes as she lay there in bewilderment. She had prepared for this moment six hours a day, every day of the week, for the past four years. The next morning, I saw her news conference. I wish I had taped it. It was amazing to listen to her perspective. She said something to the effect of "I don't know why it happened but it did, and I'm going to use it. I'm going to focus even more and work even harder for the next four years. Who knows what my path would have been had I won? Maybe it would have dulled my desire. I don't know, but I do know that now I'm hungrier than ever. I'll be back even stronger." As I heard her speak, all I could say was "Wow!" You can learn a lot from listening to champions. Rich people hang around with winners. Poor people hang around with losers. Why? It's a matter of comfort. Rich peo- ple are comfortable with other successful people. They feel fully worthy of being with them. Poor people are uncomfortable with highly successful people. They're either afraid they'll be rejected or feel as if they don't belong. To protect itself, the ego then goes into judgment and criticism. If you want to get rich, you will have to change your inner blueprint to fully believe you are every bit as good as any millionaire or multimillionaire out there. I'm shocked in my seminars when people come up to me and ask if they can touch me. They say, "I've never touched a multimillionaire before." I'm usually polite and smile, but in my mind I'm saying, "Get a frickin' life! I'm no better or different from you, and unless you start to understand that, you'll stay broke forever!" My friends, it's not about "touching" millionaires, it's about deciding that you are just as good and worthy as they are, and then acting like it. My best advice is this: if you really want to touch a millionaire, become one! I hope you get the point. Instead of mocking rich people, model them. Instead of shying away from rich people, get to know them. Instead of saying, "Wow, they're so special," say, "If they can do it, I can do it." Eventually, if you want to touch a millionaire, you'll be able to touch yourself !

1. Go to the library, a bookstore, or the Internet and read a biography of someone who is or was extremely rich and successful. Andrew Carnegie, John D. Rockefeller, Mary Kay, Donald Trump, Warren Buffett, Jack Welch, Bill Gates, and Ted Turner are some good examples. Use their story for inspiration, for learning specific success strategies, and most importantly, for copying their mind-set. 2. Join a high-end club, such as for tennis, health, business, or golf. Mingle with rich people in a rich environment. Or, if there's no way you can afford to join a high-end club, have coffee or tea in the classiest hotel in your city. Get comfortable in this atmosphere and watch the patrons, noticing they're no different from you.

3. Identify a situation or a person who is a downer in your life. Remove yourself from that situation or association. If it's family, choose to be around them less.

4. Stop watching trash TV and stay away from bad news.

Rich people are willing to promote themselves and their value. Poor people think negatively about selling and promotion. My company, AUI Training, offers over a dozen different programs. During the initial seminar, we briefly mention a few of our other courses, then offer the participants special "at seminar" tuition rates and bonuses. It's interesting to note the reactions. Most people are thrilled. They appreciate getting to hear what the other courses are about and to receive the special pricing. Some people, however, are not so thrilled. They resent any promotion regardless of how it might benefit them. If this sounds in any way like you, it's an important characteristic to notice about yourself.

Resenting promotion is one of the greatest obstacles to success. People who have issues with selling and promotion are usually broke. It's obvious. How can you create a large income in your own business or as a representative of one if you aren't willing to let people know that you, your product, or your service exists? Even as an employee, if you aren't willing to promote your virtues, someone who is willing will quickly bypass you on the corporate ladder. People have a problem with promotion or sales for several reasons. Chances are you might recognize one or more of the following. First, you may have had a bad experience in the past with people promoting to you inappropriately. Maybe you perceived they were doing the "hard" sell on you. Maybe they were bothering you at an inopportune time. Maybe they wouldn't take no for an answer. In any case, it's important to recognize that this experience is in the past and that holding on to it may not be serving you today. Second, you may have had a disempowering experience when you tried to sell something to someone and that person totally rejected you. In this instance, your distaste for promotion is merely a projection of your own fear of failure and rejection. Again, realize the past does not necessarily equal the future. Third, your issue might come from past parental programming. Many of us were told that it's impolite to "toot your own horn." Well, that's great if you make a living as Miss Manners. But in the real world, when it comes to business and money, if you don't toot your horn, I guarantee nobody will. Rich people are willing to extol their virtues and value to anyone who will listen and hopefully do business with them as well. Finally, some people feel that promotion is beneath them. I call this the high-and-mighty syndrome, otherwise known as the "Aren't I so special?" attitude. The feeling in this case is that if people want what you have, they should somehow find and come to you. People who have this belief are either broke or soon will be, that's for sure. They can hope that everyone's going to scour the land searching for them, but the truth is that the marketplace is crowded with products and services, and even though theirs may be the best, no one will ever know that because they're too snooty to tell anyone. You're probably familiar with the saying "Build a better mousetrap and the world will beat a path to your door." Well, that's only true if you add five words: "if they know about it." Rich people are almost always excellent promoters. They can and are willing to promote their products, their services, and their ideas with passion and enthusiasm. What's more, they're skilled at packaging their value in a way that's extremely attractive. If you think there's something wrong with that, then let's ban makeup for women, and while we're at it, we might as well get rid of suits for men. All that is nothing more than "packaging."Robert Kiyosaki, best-selling author of Rich Dad, Poor Dad (a book I highly recommend), points out that every business, including writing books, depends on selling. He notes that he is recognized as a best-selling author, not a best-writing author. One pays a lot more than the other. Rich people are usually leaders, and all great leaders are great promoters. To be a leader, you must inherently have followers and supporters, which means that you have to be adept at selling, inspiring, and motivating people to buy into your vision. Even the president of the United States of America has to continuously sell his ideas to the people, to Congress, and even to his own party, to have them implemented. And way before all of that takes place, if he doesn't sell himself in the first place, he'll never even get elected. In short, any leader who can't or won't promote will not be a leader for long, be it in politics, business, sports, or even as a parent. I'm harping on this because leaders earn a heck of a lot more money than followers.

Leaders earn a heck of a lot more money than followers! The critical point here isn't whether you like to promote or not, it is why you're promoting. It boils down to your beliefs. Do you really believe in your value? Do you really believe in the product or service you're offering? Do you really believe that what you have will be of benefit to whomever you're promoting it to? If you believe in your value, how could it possibly be ap-propriate to hide it from people who need it? Suppose you had a cure for arthritis, and you met someone who was suffering and in pain with the disease. Would you hide it from him or her? Would you wait for that person to read your mind or guess that you have a product that could help? What would you think of someone who didn't offer suffering people their opportunity because they were too shy, too afraid, or too cool to promote? More often than not, people who have a problem with promotion don't fully believe in their product or don't fully believe in themselves. Consequently, it's difficult for them to imagine that other people believe so strongly in their value that they want to share it with everyone who comes their way and in any way they can. If you believe that what you have to offer can truly assist people, it's your duty to let as many people as possible know about it. In this way, you not only help people, you get rich!

Rich people are bigger than their problems. Poor people are smaller than their problems. As I said earlier, getting rich is not a stroll in the park. It is a journey that is full of twists, turns, detours, and obstacles. The road to wealth is fraught with traps and pitfalls, and that's precisely why most people don't take it. They don't want the hassles, the headaches, and the responsibilities. In short, they don't want the problems. Therein lies one of the biggest differences between rich people and poor people. Rich and successful people are bigger than their problems, while poor and unsuccessful people are smaller than their problems. Poor people will do almost anything to avoid problems. They see a challenge and they run. The irony is that in their quest to make sure they don't have problems, they have the biggest problem of all... they're broke and miserable. The secret to success, my friends, is not to try to avoid or get rid of or shrink from your problems; the secret is to grow yourself so that you are bigger than any problem. The secret to success is not to try to avoid or get rid of or shrink from your problems; the secret is to grow yourself so that you are bigger than any problem. On a scale of 1 to 10, 1 being the lowest, imagine you are a person with a level 2 strength of character and attitude looking at a level 5 problem. Would this problem appear to be big or little? From a level 2 perspective, a level 5 problem would seem like a big problem. Now imagine you've grown yourself and become a level 8 person. Would the same level 5 problem be a big problem or a little problem? Magically, the identical problem is now a little problem. Finally, imagine you've really worked hard on yourself and become a level 10 person. Now, is this same level 5 problem a big problem or a little problem? The answer is that it's no problem. It doesn't even register in your brain as a problem. There's no negative energy around it. It's just a normal occurrence to handle, like brushing your teeth or getting dressed. Note that whether you are rich or poor, playing big or playing small, problems do not go away. If you're breathing, you will always have so-called problems and obstacles in your life. Let me make this short and sweet. The size of the problem is never the issue—what matters is the size of you! This may be painful, but if you're ready to move to the next level of success, you're going to have to become conscious of what's really going on in your life. Ready? Here goes. If you have a big problem in your life, all that means is that you are being a small person! Don't be fooled by appearances. Your outer world is merely a reflection of your inner world. If you want to make a permanent change, stop focusing on the size of your problems and start focusing on the size of you! One of the not-so-subtle reminders I give participants at my seminar is this: whenever you feel as if you've got a big problem, point to yourself and scream, "Mini me, mini me, mini me!" That will abruptly wake you up and move your attention back to where it belongs—on yourself. Then, coming from your "higher self " (rather than your ego-based, victim self), take a deep breath and decide right now, in this very moment, you will be a bigger person and not allow any problem or obstacle to take you out of either your happiness or success. The bigger the problems you can handle, the bigger the business you can handle; the bigger the responsibility you can handle, the more employees you can handle; the more customers you can handle, the more money you can handle, and ultimately, the more wealth you can handle. Again, your wealth can only grow to the extent that you do! The objective is to grow yourself to a place where you can overcome any problems or obstacles that get in the way of your creating wealth and keeping it once you have it. By the way, keeping your wealth is a whole other world.

Who knew? I sure didn't. I thought that once you made it, you made it! Boy, was I in for a rude awakening as I proceeded to lose my first million almost as fast as I made it. Now, in hindsight, I understand what the issue was. At the time, my "toolbox" wasn't yet big and strong enough to hold the wealth I had achieved. Again, thank goodness I practiced the principles of the Millionaire Mind and was able to recondition myself ! Not only did I make that million back, but because of my new "money blueprint," I've made millions and millions more. Best of all, I've not only kept it, but it keeps growing at a phenomenal rate! Think of yourself as your container for wealth. If your container is small and your money is big, what's going to happen? You will lose it. Your container will overflow and the excess money will spill out all over the place. You simply cannot have more money than the container. Therefore you must grow to be a big container so you cannot only hold more wealth but also attract more wealth. The universe abhors a vacuum and if you have a very large money container, it will rush in to fill the space. One of the reasons rich people are bigger than their problems goes back to what we discussed earlier. They don't focus on the problem; they focus on their goal. Again, the mind generally focuses on one predominant thing at a time. Meaning that either you are whining about the problem or you are working on the solution. Rich and successful people are solution-oriented; they spend their time and energy strategizing and planning the answers to challenges that come up, and creating systems to make certain that problem doesn't occur again. Poor and unsuccessful people are problem-oriented. They spend their time and energy bitching and complaining and seldom come up with anything creative to alleviate the problem, let alone make sure it doesn't happen again. Rich people do not back away from problems, do not avoid problems, and do not complain about problems. Rich people are financial warriors. In our Enlightened Warrior Training Camp, the definition of a warrior we use is "one who conquers oneself." The bottom line is that if you become a master at handling problems and overcoming any obstacle, what can stop you from success? The answer is nothing ! And if nothing can stop you, you become unstoppable ! And if you become unstoppable, what choices do you have in your life? The answer is all choices. If you are unstoppable, anything and everything is available to you. You simply choose it and it's yours! How's that for freedom!

Rich people are excellent receivers. Poor people are poor receivers. If I had to nail down the number one reason most people do not reach their full financial potential, it would be this: most people are poor "receivers." They may or may not be good at giving, but they are definitely bad at receiving. And because they are poor at receiving, they don't! People are challenged by receiving for several reasons. First, many people feel unworthy or undeserving. This syndrome runs rampant in our society. I would guess that over 90 percent of individuals have feelings of not being good enough running through their veins. Where does this low self-esteem come from? The usual— our conditioning. For most of us it comes from hearing twenty nos for every yes, ten "You're doing it wrong"s for every "You're doing it right," and five "You're stupid"s for every "You're awesome." Even if our parents or guardians were incredibly supportive, many of us end up with feelings of not being able to continually measure up to their accolades and expectations. So once again, we're not good enough. In addition, most of us grew up with the element of punishment in our lives. This unwritten rule simply states that if you do something wrong, you will or should be punished. Some of us were punished by our parents, some by our teachers... and some of us in certain religious circles were threatened with the mother of all punishments, not getting into heaven. Of course, now that we're adults, all this is over. Right? Wrong! For most people, the conditioning of punishment is so ingrained that, because there's no one around to punish them, when they make a mistake or just aren't perfect, they subconsciously punish themselves. When they were young, this punishment might have come in the form of "You were bad, so no candy." Today, however, it could take the form of "You were bad, so no money." This explains why some people limit their earnings, and why others will subconsciously sabotage their success. No wonder people have difficulty receiving. One tiny mistake and you're doomed to carry the burden of misery and poverty for the rest of your life. "A little harsh," you say? Since when did the mind become logical or compassionate? Again, the conditioned mind is a file folder filled with past programming, made-up meanings, and stories of drama and disaster. "Making sense" is not its strong suit. Here's something I teach in my seminars that might make you feel better. In the end, it doesn't matter whether you feel worthy or not, you can be rich either way. Plenty of wealthy people don't feel overly worthy. In fact, it's one of the major motivations for people to get rich...to prove themselves and their worth to themselves or to others. The idea that selfworth is necessary for net worth is just that, an idea, but it doesn't necessarily hold water in the real world. As we said earlier, getting rich to prove yourself may not make you the happiest camper, so you're better off creating wealth for other reasons. But what's important here is for you to realize that your feeling of unworthiness won't prevent you from getting rich; from a strictly financial point of view this could actually be a motivational asset. Having said that, I want you to get what I'm going to share with you, loud and clear. This could easily be one of the most important moments of your life. Are you ready? Here goes. Recognize that whether you are worthy or not is all a madeup "story." Again, nothing has meaning except for the meaning we give it. I don't know about you, but I've never heard of anybody who went through the "stamping" lineup at birth. Can you imagine God stamping each person's forehead as he or she came through? "Worthy...unworthy... worthy, worthy...unworthy. Yuck...definitely unworthy." Sorry, I don't think it works that way. There's no one who comes around and stamps you "worthy" or "unworthy." You do that. You make it up. You decide it. You and you alone determine if you're going to be worthy. It's simply your perspective. If you say you're worthy, you are. If you say you're not worthy, you're not. Either way you will live into your story. This is so critical, I'm going to repeat that again: you will live into your story. It's that simple. If you say you're worthy, you are. If you say you're not worthy, you're not. Either way you will live into your story. So why would people do this to themselves? Why would people make up the story that they're not worthy? It's just the nature of the human mind, the protective part of us that's always looking for what's wrong. Ever notice that a squirrel doesn't worry about these things? Can you imagine a squirrel saying, "I'm not going to collect many nuts this year to prepare for winter because I'm not worthy?" Doubtful, because these low-intelligence creatures would never do that to themselves. Only the most evolved creature on the planet, the human being, has the ability to limit itself like this. One of my own sayings is "If a hundred-foot oak tree had the mind of a human, it would only grow to be ten feet tall!" So here's my suggestion: since it's a lot easier to change your story than your worthiness, instead of worrying about changing your worthiness, change your story. It's a lot faster and cheaper. Simply make up a new and much more supportive story and live into that.

This is a special ceremony, so I'm going to ask you to eliminate any distractions right now. Stop munching, stop talking on the phone, and stop whatever you're doing. Men, if you like, you can change into a suit and tie, although a tuxedo would be best. Women, a formal evening gown and heels would be perfect. And if you don't have anything that's classy or new enough, this would definitely be an occasion to go buy yourself a brand-new dress, designer label preferred. If you're all ready, let's begin. Please kneel down on one knee and bow your head in respect. Ready, here goes. "BY THE POWER INVESTED IN ME, I HEREBY ANOINT YOU AS 'WORTHY' FROM NOW UNTIL FOREVER MORE!" Okay we're done. You can stand up now and hold your head high because you are finally worthy. Here's some sage advice: stop buying into that "worthiness" or "unworthiness" crap and start taking the actions you need to take to get rich! The second major reason most people have a problem with receiving is that they have bought into the adage "It's better to give than to receive." Let me put this as elegantly as possible: "What a crock !" That statement is total hogwash, and in case you haven't noticed, it's usually propagated by people and groups who want you to give and them to receive. The whole idea is ludicrous. What's better, hot or cold, big or small, left or right, in or out? Giving and receiving are two sides of the same coin. Whoever decided that it is better to give than to receive was simply bad at math. For every giver there must be a receiver, and for every receiver there must be a giver. For every giver there must be a receiver, and for every receiver there must be a giver. Think about it! How could you give if there weren't someone or something there to receive? Both have to be in perfect balance to work one to one, fifty-fifty. And since giving and receiving must always equal each other, they must also be equal in importance. Besides, how does it feel to give? Most of us would agree that giving feels wonderful and fulfilling. Conversely, how does it feel when you want to give and the other person isn't willing to receive? Most of us would agree that it feels terrible. So know this: if you are not willing to receive, then you are "ripping off" those who want to give to you. You are actually denying them the joy and pleasure that comes from giving; instead, they feel lousy. Why? Again, everything is energy, and when you want to give but can't, that energy cannot be expressed and gets stuck in you. That "stuck" energy then turns into negative emotions. To make matters worse, when you are not willing to fully receive, you are training the universe not to give to you! It's simple: if you aren't willing to receive your share, it will go to someone else who is. That's one of the reasons the rich get richer and the poor get poorer. Not because they're any more worthy, but because they are willing to receive while most poor people are not. I learned this lesson in a big way while camping by myself in the forest. In preparation for my two-day sojourn I made what's called a lean-to. This means tying the top part of a tarp to a tree and then fastening the bottom to the ground to create a forty-five-degree roof over my head when I slept. Thank goodness I prepared this mini-condo because it rained all night. When I came out of my shelter that morning, I was noticing how dry I and everything else under the tarp was. At the same time, however, I couldn't help but notice this unusually deep puddle that had collected at the bottom of the tarp. All of a sudden I heard this inner voice say to me, "Nature is totally abundant but not discriminating. When the rain falls, it has to go somewhere. If one part is dry, another part will be doubly wet." As I stood over the puddle, I realized this is exactly the way it works with money. There's plenty of it, trillions of trillions of dollars floating around, it's in definite abundance, and it has to go somewhere. The deal is this: if somebody isn't willing to receive his or her share, it must go to whoever will. The rain doesn't care who gets it and neither does money. At this point in the Millionaire Mind seminar I teach people the special prayer I created after my experience under the tarp. Of course it's a little tongue-in-cheek, but the lesson is obvious. It goes like this: "Universe, if anyone has something great coming to them and they're not willing to take it, send it to me! I am open and willing to receive all of your blessings. Thank you." I have the entire audience repeat this with me and they go crazy! They're excited because it feels amazing to be totally willing to receive, and it feels great because it's totally natural to do so. Anything you've made up to the contrary is, again, just a "story" that isn't serving you or anyone else. Let your story go and your money come. Rich people work hard and believe it's perfectly appropriate to be well rewarded for their efforts and the value they provide for others. Poor people work hard, but due to their feelings of unworthiness, they believe that it is inappropriate for them to be well rewarded for their efforts and the value they provide. This belief sets them up to be perfect victims, and of course, how can you be a "good" victim if you are well rewarded? Many poor people actually believe they are better people because they are poor. Somehow they believe they're more pious or spiritual or good. Baloney! The only thing poor people are, is poor. I had a gentleman at the course come to me in tears. He said, "I just don't see how I could feel good about having a lot of money when others have so little." I asked him a few simple questions: "What good do you do for poor people by being one of them? Whom do you help by being broke? Aren't you just another mouth to feed? Wouldn't it be more effective for you to create wealth for yourself and then be able to really help others from a place of strength instead of weakness?" He stopped crying and said, "For the first time, I got it. I can't believe what garbage I've been thinking. Harv, I believe the time has come for me to get rich and, along the way, help others. Thank you." He went back to his seat a new man. I got an e-mail from him not long ago telling me he's making ten times what he used to earn and that he's feeling awesome about it. Best of all, he says, it feels tremendous to be able to assist some of his friends and family who are still struggling. This leads me to an important point: if you have the wherewithal to have a lot of money, have it. Why? Because the truth is that we are extremely fortunate to be living in this society, a society whereby each person is in fact rich compared to many other parts of the world. Some people just don't ever have the opportunity to have a lot of money. If you are one of the lucky people who do have that ability, and each of you is or you wouldn't be reading a book like this, then use your wherewithal for all it's worth. Get really rich and then help people who don't have the opportunity you did. That makes a lot more sense to me than being broke and helping no one. Of course there are the people who will say, "Money will change me. If I get rich, I might turn into some kind of greedy jerk." First, the only people who say that are poor people. It's just another justification for their failure, and it comes from just another one of the many "inner" weeds in their financial garden. Don't buy it! Second, let me set the record straight. Money will only make you more of what you already are. If you're mean, money will afford you the opportunity to be meaner. If you're kind, money will afford you the opportunity to be kinder. If you're a jerk at heart, with money you can be jerkier. (I know there's no such word, but if you were a real jerk, you'd find a way.) If you're generous, more money will simply allow you to be more generous. And anyone who tells you different is broke

!

Money will only make you more of what you already are. So what to do? How do you become a good receiver? First, begin to nurture yourself. Remember, people are creatures of habit, and therefore you will have to consciously practice receiving the best life has to offer. One of the key elements in the money management system we teach in the Millionaire Mind Intensive Seminar is having a "play" account where you get to blow a designated amount of money on things that nurture you and allow you to "feel like a million." The idea of this account is to help you validate your worthiness and strengthen your "receiving muscle." Second, I want you to practice going crazy with excitement and gratitude anytime you find or receive any money. It's funny, when I was broke and I saw a penny on the ground, I would never stoop so low as to pick up a lowly penny. Now that I'm rich, however, I pick up anything that even looks like money. Then I give it a kiss for good luck and declare out loud, "I am a money magnet. Thank you, thank you, thank you." I don't stand there judging the denomination. Money is money, and finding money is a blessing from the universe. Now that I'm fully willing to receive anything and everything that comes my way, I do! Being open and willing to receive is absolutely critical if you want to create wealth. It's also critical if you want to keep it. If you are a poor receiver and you somehow fall into a substantial amount of money, chances are it'll be gone quickly. Again, "first the inner, then the outer." First, expand your receiving "box." Then watch as the money comes in to fill it. Again, the universe abhors a vacuum. In other words, an empty space will always be filled. Have you ever noticed what happens with an empty closet or garage? It usually doesn't stay empty for long, does it? Have you also noticed how strange it is that the time taken for any task will always be equal to the time given? Once you expand your capacity to receive, you will. Also, once you become truly open to receiving, the rest of your life will open up. Not only will you receive more money, but you'll also receive more love, more peace, more happiness, and more fulfillment. Why? Because of another principle I constantly use that states, "How you do anything is how you do everything."

How you do anything is how you do everything. The way you are in one area is usually the way you are in all areas. If you've been blocking yourself from receiving money, chances are you've been blocking yourself from receiving everything else that's good in life. The mind doesn't usually delineate specifically where you are a poor receiver. In fact, it's just the opposite: the mind has a habit of overgeneralizing and says, "The way it is, is the way it is, everywhere and always." If you're a poor receiver, you're a poor receiver in all areas. The good news is that when you become an excellent receiver, you'll be an excellent receiver everywhere...and open to receiving all that the universe has to offer in all areas of your life. Now the only thing you'll have to remember is to keep saying "Thank you" as you receive all of your blessings.Rich people choose to get paid based on results. Poor people choose to get paid based on time. Have you ever heard this advice: "Go to school, get good grades, get a good job, get a steady paycheck, be on time, work hard . . . and you'll live happily ever after"? I don't know about you, but I'd sure love to see the written guarantee on that one. Unfortunately, this sage advice comes directly from the Book of Fairy Tales, Volume I, right after the tooth fairy story. I'm not going to bother debunking the entire statement. You can do that for yourself by checking your own experience and the lives of everyone around you. What I will discuss is the idea behind the "steady" paycheck. There's nothing wrong with getting a steady paycheck, unless it interferes with your ability to earn what you're worth. There's the rub. It usually does.Poor people prefer to be paid a steady salary or hourly wage. They need the "security" of knowing that exactly the same amount of money is coming in at exactly the same time, month in, month out. What they don't realize is that this security comes with a price, and the cost is wealth. Living based in security is living based in fear. What you're actually saying is "I'm afraid I won't be able to earn enough based on my performance, so I'll settle for earning just enough to survive or to be comfortable." Rich people prefer to get paid based on the results they produce, if not totally, then at least partially. Rich people usually own their own business in some form. They make their income from their profits. Rich people work on commission or percentages of revenue. Rich people choose stock options and profit sharing in lieu of higher salaries. Notice there are no guarantees with any of the above. As stated earlier, in the financial world the rewards are usually proportionate to the risk. Rich people believe in themselves. They believe in their value and in their ability to deliver it. Poor people don't. That's why they need "guarantees." Recently, I dealt with a public relations consultant who wanted me to pay her a fee of $4,000 per month. I asked her what I'd receive for my $4,000. She replied that I'd see at least $20,000 of coverage per month in the media. I said, "What if you don't produce those results or anything close to it?" She answered that she would still be putting in the time, so she deserved to get paid. I replied, "I'm not interested in paying for your time.

I'm interested in paying you for a specific result, and if you don't produce that result, why should I pay you? On the other hand, if you produce even greater results, you should get paid more. Tell you what: I'll give you fifty percent of whatever media value you produce. According to your figures, that would mean paying you ten thousand dollars per month, which is more than double your fee." Did she go for it? Nope! Is she broke? Yup! And she will be for the rest of her life or until she figures out that to get rich you will need to be paid based on results. Poor people trade their time for money. The problem with this strategy is that your time is limited. This means that you invariably end up breaking Wealth Rule #1, which states, "Never have a ceiling on your income." If you choose to get paid for your time, you are pretty much killing your chances for wealth.Never have a ceiling on your income. This rule also applies to personal service businesses, where, again, you generally get paid for your time. That's why lawyers, accountants, and consultants who are not yet partners in their firm—and therefore don't share in the business profits—make a moderate living at best. Suppose you are in the pen business and you get an order for fifty thousand pens. If this were the case, what would you do? You'd simply call your supplier, order fifty thousand pens, send them off, and happily count your profits. On the other hand, suppose you are a massage therapist and you're fortunate enough to have fifty thousand people lined up outside your door all wanting a massage from you. What do you do? You kill yourself for not being in the pen business. What else can you do? Try explaining to the last person in line that you may be running "a little late," as in their appointment is Tuesday at 3:15, four decades from now . I'm not suggesting there's anything wrong with being in a personal service business. Just don't expect to get rich anytime soon unless you create a way to duplicate or leverage yourself. At my seminars, I often meet salaried or hourly wage employees who complain to me that they're not getting paid what they're worth. My response is "In whose opinion? I'm sure your boss thinks you're being compensated fairly. Why don't you get off the salary treadmill and ask to be paid based fully or partially on your performance? Or, if that is not possible, why not work for yourself ? Then you'll know you're making exactly what you're worth." Somehow, this advice doesn't seem to appease these people, who are obviously terrified of testing their "true" value in the marketplace. The fear most people have of being paid based on their results is often just a fear of breaking out of their old conditioning. In my experience, most people who are stuck in the steady-paycheck rut have past programming that tells them this is the "normal" way to get paid for your work. You can't blame your parents. (I guess you can if you're a good victim.) Most parents tend to be overly protective, so it's only natural for them to want their kids to have a secure existence. As you've probably already found out, any work that doesn't provide a steady paycheck usually produces the infamous parental response "When are you going to get a real job?" I remember, when my parents asked me that question, thank goodness my reply was "Hopefully never!" My mother was devastated. My father, however, said, "Good for you. You'll never get rich working on straight salary for someone else. If you're going to get a job, make sure you get paid on percentage. Otherwise, go work for yourself !"I too encourage you to work "for yourself." Start your own business, work on commission, get a percentage of revenue or company profits, or get stock options. Whatever your vehicle, make certain you create a situation that allows you to get paid based on your results. Personally, I believe just about everyone should own their own business, be it full-time or part-time. The first reason is that by far, the vast majority of millionaires became rich by being in their own business. Secondly, it's extremely difficult to create wealth when the tax man is grabbing almost half of everything you earn. When you own a business, you can save a small fortune in taxes by writing off a portion of your expenses for such things as your car, travel, education, and even your home. For that reason alone, it's worth having your own business. If you don't have a brilliant business idea, not to worry: you can use someone else's. First, you can become a commissioned salesperson. Selling is one of the world's highest-paid professions. If you're good, you can earn a fortune. Second, you can join a network marketing company. There are dozens of excellent ones, and they have in place all of the products and systems you need to get started immediately. For just a few bucks, you can become a distributor and have all the benefits of owning a business with few of the administrative hassles. If it resonates with you, network marketing can be a dynamite vehicle for wealth. But, and this is a big but, don't think for a minute that you're going to get a free ride. Network marketing will only work if you do. It will take training, time, and energy to succeed. But if you do, incomes in the range of $20,000 to $50,000 per month—that's right, per month—are not uncommon. In any case, just signing up and becoming a part-time distributor will give you some excellent tax advantages, and who knows, maybe you'll enjoy the product enough to offer it to others and end up making a nice income to boot. Another option is exchanging your "job" for a "contract" position. If your employer is willing, he or she can hire your company instead of you to do basically what you're doing now. A few legal requirements have to be fulfilled, but for the most part, if you add one or two more clients, even part-time, you can get paid as a business owner instead of an employee and enjoy business-owner tax benefits. Who knows, those parttime clients may grow to become full-time clients, which would then give you the opportunity to leverage yourself, hire other people to get all the work done, and eventually you'll be running your own full-on business. You might think, "My employer would never go for that." I wouldn't be too sure about that. You have to understand, it costs a company a fortune to have an employee. Not only do they have to pay salary or wages, but they have to pay a whack of money on top of that to the government, often to the tune of 25 percent or more above what the employee earns. Add to that the cost of the benefits package that most employees get, and you've probably got a 50 percent savings to a company that chooses to hire you as an independent consultant. Of course you won't be eligible for many of the benefits you got as an employee, but for what you save in taxes alone, you can buy the best of what you need on your own. In the end, the only way to earn what you're really worth is to get paid based on your results. Once again, my dad said it best: "You'll never get rich working on straight salary for someone else. If you're going to get a job, make sure you get paid on percentage. Otherwise, go work for yourself !" Now that's sage advice!

Rich people live in a world of abundance. Poor people live in a world of limitations. Of course, both live in the same physical world, but the difference is in their perspective. Poor and most middle-class people come from scarcity. They live by mottos such as "There's only so much to go around, there's never enough, and you can't have everything." And although you may not be able to have "everything," as in all the things in the world, I do think you can certainly have "everything you really want." Do you want a successful career or a close relationship with your family? Both! Do you want to focus on business or have fun and play? Both! Do you want money or meaning in your life? Both! Do you want to earn a fortune or do the work you love? Both! Poor people always choose one, rich people choose both. Rich people understand that with a little creativity you can almost always figure out a way to have the best of both worlds. From now on, when confronted with an either/or alternative, the quintessential question to ask yourself is "How can I have both?" This question will change your life. It will take you from a model of scarcity and limitation to a universe of possibilities and abundance. This doesn't just pertain to things you want, it pertains to all areas of life. For example, right now, I'm preparing to deal with an unhappy supplier that believes my company, Peak Potentials, should pay for certain expenses they've had that weren't originally agreed to. My feeling is that estimat-ing his costs is his business not mine, and if he's incurred higher expenses, that's something he has to deal with. I'm more than willing to negotiate a new agreement for next time, but I'm big on keeping agreements that were already made. Now in my "broke" days, I'd go into this discussion with the goal of making my point and making sure I don't pay this guy one cent more than we agreed upon. And even though I'd like to keep him as a supplier, this would probably end up in a huge argument. I'd go in thinking either he wins or I win. Today, however, because I've trained myself to think in terms of "both," I'm going into this discussion completely open to creating a situation where I'm not going to pay him any more money and he's going to be extremely happy with the arrangements we do make. In other words, my goal is to have both ! Here's another example. Several months ago I decided to purchase a vacation home in Arizona. I scoured the area I was interested in, and every real estate agent told me, if I wanted three bedrooms plus a den in that vicinity, I'd have to pay over a million dollars. My intention was to keep my investment in this home under a million. Most people would either lower their expectations or raise their budget. I held out for both. I recently got a call that the owners of a house in the exact location I wanted, with the number of rooms I wanted, had reduced their price $200,000 to under a million. Here is another tribute to the intention of having both! Finally, I always told my parents that I didn't want to slave away at work I didn't enjoy and that I would "get rich doing what I love." Their response was the usual: "You're living in a dream world. Life is not a bowl of cherries." They said, "Business is business, pleasure is pleasure. First you take care of making a living, then, if there's any time left over, you can enjoy your life." I remember thinking to myself, "Hmm, if I listen to them, I'll end up like them. No. I'm gonna have both!" Was it tough? You bet. Sometimes I'd have to work at a job I hated for a week or two so I could eat and pay the rent. But I never lost my intention of having "both." I never got stuck long-term in a job or business I didn't like. Eventually I did become rich doing what I loved. Now that I know it can be done, I continue to pursue only the work and projects that I love. Best of all, I now have the privilege of teaching others to do the same. Nowhere is "both" thinking more important than when it comes to money. Poor and many middle-class people believe that they have to choose between money and the other aspects of life. Consequently they've rationalized a position that money is not as important as other things. Let's set the record straight. Money is important! To say that it's not as important as any of the other things in life is ludicrous. What's more important, your arm or your leg? Could it be that both are important? Money is a lubricant. It enables you to "slide" through life instead of having to "scrape" by. Money brings freedom— freedom to buy what you want, and freedom to do what you want with your time. Money allows you to enjoy the finer things in life as well as giving you the opportunity to help others have the necessities in life. Most of all, having money allows you not to have to spend your energy worrying about not having money. Happiness is important too. Again, here's where poor and middle-class people get confused. Many believe money and happiness are mutually exclusive, that either you can be rich or you can be happy. Again, this is nothing more than "poor" programming. People who are rich in every sense of the word understand that you have to have both. Just as you have to have both your arms and your legs, you have to have money and happiness. So here's another major difference between rich people, middle-class people, and poor people: Rich people believe "You can have your cake and eat it too." Middle-class people believe "Cake is too rich, so I'll only have a little piece." Poor people don't believe they deserve cake, so they order a doughnut, focus on the hole, and wonder why they have "nothing." Rich people believe "You can have your cake and eat it too." Middle-class people believe "Cake is too rich, so I'll only have a little piece." Poor people don't believe they deserve cake, so they order a doughnut, focus on the hole, and wonder why they have "nothing." I ask you, what is the use of having your "cake" if you can't eat it? What exactly are you supposed to do with it? Put it on your mantel and look at it? Cake is meant to be eaten and enjoyed. Either/or thinking also trips up people who believe that "if I have more, then someone else will have less." Again, this is nothing more than fear-based, self-defeating programming. The notion that the wealthy people of the world have and are somehow hoarding all the money, so there's none left for anyone else, is preposterous. First, this belief assumes that there is a limited supply of money. I'm not an economist, but from what I can see, they just keep printing more of the stuff every day. The actual money supply hasn't been tied to any real asset for decades. So even if the wealthy had all the money today, tomorrow there'd be millions, if not billions, more available. The other thing people with this limited belief don't seem to realize is that the same money can be used over and over, to create value for everyone. Let me give you an example I've used in our seminars. I'll ask five people to come onstage and bring an item with them. I ask them to stand in a circle. Then I give a $5 bill to the first person and ask them to buy something from person number 2 for that money. Suppose they buy a pen. So now person number 1 has a pen and person number 2 has the $5. Person 2 now uses the same $5 bill to buy, say, a clipboard from person number 3. Then number 3 uses the same $5 bill to buy a notebook from number 4. I hope you get the picture and the point. The exact same $5 was used to bring value to each person that had it. That same $5 went through five different people and created $5 worth of value for each and a total of $25 in value for the group. That $5 did not get depleted and as it circled around, created value for everyone.The lessons are clear. First, money does not get depleted; you can use the same money again and again for years and years and thousands and thousands of people. Second, the more money you have, the more you can put into the circle, which means other people then have more money to trade for more value. This is exactly the opposite of either/or-based thinking. To the contrary, when you have money and use it, you and the person you spend it with both have the value. Put bluntly, if you're so worried about other people and making sure they get their share (as if there is a share), do what it takes to get rich so you can spread more money around. If I can be an example for anything, it would be that you can be a kind, loving, caring, generous, and spiritual person and be really frickin' rich. I strongly urge you to dispel the myth that money is in any way bad or that you will be less "good" or less "pure" if you are wealthy. That belief is absolute "salami" (in case you're tired of baloney), and if you keep eating it, you won't just be fat, you'll be fat and broke. Hey, what do you know, another example of both! My friends, being kind, generous, and loving has nothing to do with what is or isn't in your wallet. Those attributes come from what is in your heart. Being pure and spiritual have nothing to do with what is or isn't in your bank account; those attributes come from what's in your soul. To think money makes you good or bad, one way or another, is either/or thinking and just plain "programmed garbage" that is not supportive to your happiness and success. It's also not supportive to those around you, especially to children. If you're that adamant about being a good person, then be "good" enough not to infect the next generation with the disempowering beliefs you may inadvertently have adopted. If you really want to live a life without limits, whatever the situation, let go of either/or thinking and maintain the intention to have "both."

Rich people focus on their net worth. Poor people focus on their working income. When it comes to money, people in our society typically ask, "How much do you make?" Seldom do you hear the ques-tion "What is your net worth?" Few people talk this way, except of course at the country club. In country clubs, the financial discussion almost always centers around net worth: "Jim just sold his stock options; he's worth over three million. Paul's company just went public; he's worth eight million. Sue just sold her business; she's now worth twelve million." At the country club, you're not going to hear, "Hey, did you hear that Joe got a raise? Yeah, and a two percent cost-of-living allowance to boot?" If you did hear that, you'd know you're listening to a guest for the day.The true measure of wealth is net worth, not working income. The true measure of wealth is net worth, not working income. Always has been, always will be. Net worth is the financial value of everything you own. To determine your net worth, add up the value of everything you own, including your cash and investments such as stocks, bonds, real estate, the current value of your business if you own one, the value of your residence if you own it, and then subtract everything you owe. Net worth is the ultimate measure of wealth because, if necessary, what you own can eventually be liquidated into cash. Rich people understand the huge distinction between working income and net worth. Working income is important, but it is only one of the four factors that determine your net worth. The four net worth factors are:1. Income 2. Savings 3. Investments 4. Simplification Rich people understand that building a high net worth is an equation that contains all four elements. Because all of these factors are essential, let's examine each one. Income comes in two forms: working income and passive income. Working income is the money earned from active work. This includes a paycheck from a day-to-day job, or for an entrepreneur, the profits or income taken from a business. Working income requires that you are investing your own time and labor to earn money. Working income is important because, without it, it is almost impossible to address the other three net worth factors. Working income is how we fill up our financial "funnel," so to speak. All things being equal, the more working income you earn, the more you can save and invest. Although working income is critical, again it is only valuable as a part of the entire net worth equation. Unfortunately, poor and many middle-class people focus exclusively on working income, out of the four factors. Consequently, they end up with a low or no net worth.

Passive income is money earned without you actively working. We will discuss passive income in greater detail a little later, but for now, consider it another stream of income filling up the funnel, which can then be used for spending, saving, and investing. Savings is also imperative. You can earn wads of money. But if you don't keep any of it, you will never create wealth. Many people have a financial blueprint that is wired for spending. Whatever money they have, they spend. They choose immediate gratification over long-term balance. Spenders have three mottoes. Their first motto is "It's only money." Therefore, money is something they don't have much of. Their second motto is "What goes around, comes around." At least they hope so, because their third motto is "Sorry, I can't right now. I'm broke." Without creating income to fill the funnel and savings to keep it there, it is impossible to address the next net worth factor. Once you've begun saving a decent portion of your income, then you can move to the next stage and make your money grow through investing. Generally, the better you are at investing, the faster your money will grow and generate a greater net worth. Rich people take the time and energy to learn about investing and investments. They pride themselves on being excellent investors or at least hiring excellent investors to invest for them. Poor people think investing is only for rich people, so they never learn about it and stay broke. Again, every part of the equation is important. Our fourth net worth factor may well be the "dark horse" of the bunch, because few people recognize its importance in creating wealth. This is the factor of "simplification." It goes hand in hand with saving money, whereby you consciously create a lifestyle in which you need less money to live on. By decreasing your cost of living, you increase your savings and the amount of funds available for investing. To illustrate the power of simplification, here's the story of one of our Millionaire Mind participants. When Sue was only twenty-three, she made a wise choice: she purchased a home. She paid just under $300,000 at the time. Seven yearslater, in a sizzling hot market, Sue sold her home for over $600,000, meaning she profited over $300,000. She considered buying a new home, but after attending the Millionaire Mind Intensive Seminar, she recognized that if she invested her money in a secure second mortgage at 10 percent interest and simplified her lifestyle, she could actually be quite comfortable living on the earnings from her investments and not have to work ever again. Instead of purchasing a new home, she moved in with her sister. Now, at thirty years of age, Sue is financially free. She won her independence not through earning a ton of money, but by consciously scaling back her personal overhead. Yes, she still works—because she enjoys it—but she doesn't have to. In fact, she only works six months of the year. The rest of the time she spends in Fiji, first because she loves it, and second, she says, her money goes even further there. Because she lives with the locals rather than the tourists, she doesn't spend a lot. How many people do you know who would love to spend six months of each year living on a tropical island, never having to work again, at the ripe old age of thirty? How about forty? Fifty? Sixty? Ever? It's all because Sue created a simple lifestyle and, consequently, doesn't need a fortune to live on. So, what will it take for you to be happy financially? If you need to live in a mansion, have three vacation homes, own ten cars, take annual trips around the world, eat caviar, and drink the finest champagne to enjoy your life, that's fine, but recognize you've set your bar pretty darn high, and it may take you a long, long time to get to a point where you're happy. On the other hand, if you don't need all the "toys" to be happy, you'll probably reach your financial goal a lot sooner. Again, building your net worth is a four-part equation. As an analogy, imagine driving a bus with four wheels. What would the ride be like if you were driving on one wheel only? Probably slow, bumpy, full of struggle, sparks, and going in circles. Does that sound familiar? Rich people play the money game on all four wheels. That's why their ride is fast, smooth, direct, and relatively easy. By the way, I use the analogy of a bus because once you are successful, your goal might be to bring others along on the ride with you. Poor and most middle-class people play the money game on one wheel only. They believe that the only way to get rich is to earn a lot of money. They believe that only because they've never been there. They don't understand Parkinson's Law, which states, "Expenses will always rise in direct proportion to income." Here's what's normal in our society. You have a car, you make more money, and you get a better car. You have a house, you make more money, and you get a bigger house. You have clothes, you make more money, and you get nicer clothes. You have holidays, you make more money, and you spend more on holidays. Of course there are a few exceptions to this rule...very few! In general, as income goes up, expenses almost invariably go up too. That's why income alone will never create wealth. This book is called Secrets of the Millionaire Mind. Does millionaire refer to income or net worth? Net worth. Therefore, if your intention is to be a millionaire or more, you must focus on building your net worth, which, as we've discussed, is based on much more than just your income. Make it a policy to know your net worth to the penny. Here's an exercise that can change your financial life forever. Take a blank sheet of paper and title it "Net Worth." Then create a simple chart that begins with zero and ends with whatever your net worth objective is. Note your current net worth as it is today. Then every ninety days, enter your new net worth. That's it. If you do this, you will find yourself getting richer and richer. Why? Because you will be "tracking" your net worth. "Where attention goes, energy flows and results show." By tracking your worth, you are focusing on it, and because what you focus on expands, your net worth will expand. By the way, this law goes for every other part of your life: what you track increases. To that end, I encourage you to find and work with a good financial planner. These professionals can help you track and build your net worth. They will assist you in organizing your finances and introduce you to a variety of vehicles for saving and growing your money. The best way to find a good planner is to seek a referral from a friend or associate who is happy with the person he or she uses. I'm not saying to take everything your planner says as gospel. But I am suggesting that you find a qualified professional with the skills to help you plan and track your finances. A good planner can provide you with the tools, software, knowledge, and recommendations to help you build the kind of investing habits that will produce wealth. Generally, I recommend finding a planner who works with an array of financial products rather than just insurance or just mutual funds. In that way, you can find out about a variety of options, then decide what's right for you. Rich people manage their money well. Poor people mismanage their money well. Thomas Stanley, in his best-selling book, The Millionaire Next Door, surveyed millionaires from across North America and reported on who they are and how they attained their wealth. The results can be summarized in one short sentence: "Rich people are good at managing their money." Rich people manage their money well. Poor people mismanage their money. Wealthy people are not any smarter than poor people; they just have different and more supportive money habits. As we discussed in Part I of this book, these habits are primarily based on our past conditioning. So first, if you're not managing your money properly, you were probably programmed not to manage money. Second, there's a better than good chance you don't know how to manage your money in a way that's easy and effective. I don't know about you, but where I went to school, Money Management 101 wasn't offered. Instead we learned about the War of 1812, which of course is something I use every single day. It may not be the most glamorous of topics, but it comes down to this: the single biggest difference between financial success and financial failure is how well you manage your money. It's simple: to master money, you must manage money. Poor people either mismanage their money or they avoid the subject of money altogether. Many people don't like to manage their money because, first, they say it restricts their freedom, and second, they say they don't have enough money to manage. As for the first excuse, managing money does not restrict your freedom—to the contrary, it promotes it. Managing your money allows you to eventually create financial freedom so that you never have to work again. To me, that's real freedom. As for those who use the "I don't have enough money to manage" rationale, they're looking through the wrong end of the telescope. Rather than say "when I have plenty of money, I'll begin to manage it," the reality is "when I begin to manage it, I'll have plenty of money." Saying "I'll start managing my money as soon as I get caught up" is like an overweight person saying "I'll start exercising and dieting as soon as I lose twenty pounds." It's putting the cart before the horse, which leads to going nowhere...or even backward! First you start properly handling the money you have, then you'll have more money to handle. In the Millionaire Mind Intensive Seminar, I tell a story that hits most people right between the eyes. Imagine you're walking along the street with a five-year-old. You come across an ice cream store and go inside. You get the child a single scoop of ice cream on a cone because they don't have any cups. As the two of you walk outside, you notice the cone wobbling in the child's tiny hands and, all of a sudden, plop. The ice cream falls out of the cone onto the pavement. The child begins to cry. So back you go into the store, and just as you're about to order for the second time, the child notices a colorful sign with a picture of the "triple scooper" cone. The child points to the picture and excitedly screams, "I want that one!"

The habit of managing your money is more important than the amount. So how exactly do you manage your money? At the Millionaire Mind Intensive Seminar, we teach what many believe to be an amazingly simple and effective money man-agement method. It's beyond the scope of this book to go over every detail; however, let me give you a couple of the basics so you can get started. Open a separate bank account designated your Financial Freedom Account. Put 10 percent of every dollar you receive (after taxes) into this fund. This money is only to be used for investments and buying or creating passive-income streams. The job of this account is to build a golden goose that lays golden eggs called passive income. And when do you get to spend this money? Never! It is never spent—only invested.

Eventually, when you retire, you get to spend the income from the fund (the eggs), but never the principal itself. In this way, it always keeps growing and you can never go broke. One of our students, named Emma, recently told me her story. Two years ago Emma was about to claim bankruptcy. She didn't want to; however, she felt she had no other option. She was in debt beyond what she could handle. Then she attended the Millionaire Mind Intensive Seminar and learned about the money management system. Emma said, "This is it. This is how I'm going to get out of this mess!" Emma, like all the participants, was told to divide her money into several different accounts. "That's just great," she thought to herself. "I don't have any money to divide up!" But since she wanted to try, Emma decided to divide up $1 a month into the accounts. Yes, that's right, only $1 a month. Based on the allocation system we teach, using that one dollar, she put ten cents into her FFA (Financial Freedom Account). The first thing she thought to herself was "How the heck am I supposed to become financially free on ten cents a month?" So she committed to doubling that dollar every month. The second month she divided up $2, the third month $4, then $8, $16, $32, $64, and so on until the twelfth month was $2,048 that she was dividing up each month. Then, two years later, she began to collect some amazing fruits from her efforts. She was able to put $10,000 directly into her Financial Freedom Account! She had developed the habit of managing her money so well that, when a bonus check of $10,000 came her way, she didn't need the money for anything else! Emma is now out of debt and on her way to becoming financially free. All because she took action with what she'd learned, even if it was only with $1 a month. It doesn't matter if you have a fortune right now or virtually nothing. What does matter is that you immediately begin to manage what you've got, and you'll be in shock at how soon you get more. I had another student at the Millionaire Mind Intensive Seminar say, "How can I manage my money when I'm borrowing money to live on as it is?" The answer is, borrow an extra dollar and manage that dollar. Even if you are borrowing or finding just a few dollars a month, you must manage that money, because more than a "physical" world principle is at play here: this is also a spiritual principle. Money miracles will occur once you demonstrate to the universe that you can handle your finances properly. In addition to opening a Financial Freedom bank account, create a Financial Freedom jar in your home and deposit money into it every day. It could be $10, $5, $1, a single penny, or all your loose change. The amount doesn't matter; the habit does. The secret again is to place daily "attention" on your objective of becoming financially free. Like attracts like, money attracts more money. Let this simple jar become your "money magnet," attracting more and more money and opportunities for financial freedom into your life. Now, I'm sure this isn't the first time you've heard the advice to save 10 percent of your money for long-term investing, but it may be the first time you've heard that you must have an equal and opposite account specifically designed for you to "blow" money and play. One of the biggest secrets to managing money is balance. On one side, you want to save as much money as possible so you can invest it and make more money. On the other side, you need to put another 10 percent of your income into a "play" account. Why? Because we are holistic in nature. You cannot affect one part of your life without affecting the others. Some people save, save, save, and while their logical and responsible self is fulfilled, their "inner spirit" is not. Eventually this "fun-seeking" spirit side will say, "I've had enough. I want some attention too," and sabotage their results. On the other hand, if you spend, spend, spend, not only will you never become rich, but the responsible part of you will eventually create the situation where you don't even enjoy the things you spend your money on, and you'll end up feeling guilty. The guilt will then cause you to unconsciously overspend as a way of expressing your emotions. Although you might feel better temporarily, soon it's back to guilt and shame. It's a vicious cycle, and the only way to prevent it is to learn how to manage your money in a way that works. Your play account is primarily used to nurture yourself— to do the things you wouldn't normally do. It's for the extraspecial things like going to a restaurant and ordering a bottle of their finest wine or champagne. Or renting a boat for the day. Or staying in a high-class hotel for an extravagant night of fun and frolic. The play account rule is that it must be spent every month. That's right! Each month you have to blow all the money in that account in a way that makes you feel rich. For example, imagine walking into a massage center, dumping all the money from your account on the counter, pointing to the massage therapists, and saying, "I want both of you on me. With the hot rocks and the frickin' cucumbers. After that, bring me lunch!" Like I said, extravagant. The only way most of us will ever continue to follow our saving plan is by offsetting it with a playing plan that will reward us for our efforts. Your play account is also designed to strengthen your "receiving" muscle. It also makes managing money a heck of a lot more fun. In addition to the play account and the financial freedom account, I advise that you create four more accounts. The other accounts include: 10 percent into your

Long-Term Savings for Spending Account 10 percent into your Education Account 50 percent into your Necessities Account 10 percent into your Give Account Again, poor people think it's all about income; they believe you have to earn a fortune to get rich. Again, that's male-cow manure! The fact is that if you manage your money following this program, you can become financially free on a relatively small income. If you mismanage your money, you can't become financially free, even on a huge in come. That is why so many high-income professionals— doctors, lawyers, athletes, and even accountants—are basically broke, because it's not just about what comes in, it's about what you do with what comes in. One of our attendees, John, told me that when he first heard about the money management system, he thought, "How boring! Why would anyone spend their precious time doing that?" Then later during the seminar he finally realized if he wanted to be financially free someday, especially sooner than later, he too would have to manage his money, just like the rich. John had to learn this new habit because it definitely wasn't natural for him. He said it reminded him of when he was training for triathlons. He was really good at swimming and cycling; however, he hated the running. It hurt his feet, knees, and back. He was stiff after every training session. He was always out of breath and his lungs burned every time, even if he wasn't going fast! He used to dread running. However, he knew that if he was to become a top triathlete, he had to learn to run and accept it as part of what it took to succeed. Whereas in the past John avoided running, he now decided to run every day. After a few months, he began enjoying running and actually looked forward to it each day.

Either you control money, or it will control you. I love hearing seminar graduates share how much more confident they feel around money, success, and themselves once they begin managing their money properly. The best part is that this confidence transfers into other parts of their lives and enhances their happiness, their relationships, and even their health. Money is a big part of your life, and when you learn how to get your finances under control, all areas of your life will soar.

Rich people have their money work hard for them. Poor people work hard for their money. If you're like most people, you grew up being programmed that you "have to work hard for money." Chances are good, however, that you didn't grow up with the conditioning that it was just as important to make your money "work hard for you." No question, working hard is important, but working hard alone will never make you rich. How do we know that? Take a look in the real world. There are millions—no, make that billions—of people who slave away, working their tails off all day and even all night long. Are they all rich? No! Are most of them rich? No! Are a lot of them rich? No! Most of them are broke or close to it. On the other hand, whom do you see lounging around the country clubs of the world? Who spends their afternoons playing golf, tennis, or sailing? Who spends their days shopping and their weeks vacationing? I'll give you three guesses and the first two don't count. Rich people, that's who! So let's get this straight: the idea that you have to work hard to get rich is bogus! The old Protestant work ethic states "a dollar's work for a dollar's pay." There's nothing wrong with that adage except that they forgot to tell us what to do with that "dollar's pay." Knowing what to do with that dollar is where you move from hard work to smart work. Rich people can spend their days playing and relaxing because they work smart. They understand and use leverage. They employ other people to work for them and their money to work for them. Yes, in my experience, you do have to work hard for your money. For rich people, however, this is a temporary situation. For poor people, it's permanent. Rich people understand that "you" have to work hard until your "money" works hard enough to take your place. They understand that the more your money works, the less you will have to work. Remember, money is energy. Most people put work energy in and get money energy out. People who achieve financial freedom have learned how to substitute their investment of work energy with other forms of energy. These forms include other people's work, business systems at work, or investment capital at work. Again, first you work hard for money, then you let money work hard for you. When it comes to the money game, most people don't have a clue as to what it takes to win. What's your goal? When do you win the game? Are you shooting for three square meals a day, $100,000 a year in income, becoming a millionaire, becoming a multimillionaire? At the Millionaire Mind Intensive Seminar, the goal of the money game we teach is to "never have to work again... unless you choose to," and that if you work, you work "by choice, not by necessity." In other words, the goal is to become "financially free" as quickly as possible. My definition of financial freedom is simple: it is the ability to live the lifestyle you desire without having to work or rely on anyone else for money. Notice there is a good chance that your desired lifestyle is going to cost money. Therefore, to be "free," you will need to earn money without working. We refer to income without work as passive income. To win the money game, the goal is to earn enough passive income to pay for your desired lifestyle. In short, you become financially free when your passive income exceeds your expenses. I have identified two primary sources of passive income. The first is "money working for you." This includes investment earnings from financial instruments such as stocks, bonds, T-bills, money markets, mutual funds, as well as owning mortgages or other assets that appreciate in value and can be liquidated for cash. The second major source of passive income is "business working for you." This entails generating ongoing income from businesses where you do not need to be personally involved for that business to operate and yield an income. Examples include rental real estate; royalties from books, music, or software; licensing your ideas; becoming a franchisor; owning storage units; owning vending or other types of coin-operated machines; and network marketing, to name just a few. It also includes setting up any business under the sun or moon that is systematized to work without you. Again, it's a matter of energy. The idea is that the business is working and producing value for people, instead of you.Network marketing, for example, is an amazing concept. First, it doesn't usually require you to put up a lot of up-front capital. Second, once you've done the initial work, it allows you to enjoy ongoing residual income (another form of income without you working), year after year after year. Try creating that from a regular nine-to-five job! I can't overemphasize the importance of creating passive income structures. It's simple. Without passive income you can never be free. But, and it's a big but, did you know that most people have a tough time creating passive income? There are three reasons. First, conditioning. Most of us were actually programmed not to earn passive income. When you were somewhere between thirteen and sixteen years old and you needed money, what did your parents tell you? Did they say, "Well, go out there and earn some passive income?" Doubtful! Most of us heard, "Go to work," "Go get a job," or something to that effect. We were taught to "work" for money, making passive income abnormal for most of us. Second, most of us were never taught how to earn passive income. In my school, Passive Income 101 was another subject that was never offered. This time I got to take woodworking and metalworking (notice both still entailed "working") and make the perfect candleholder for my mom. Since we didn't learn about creating passive income structures in school, we learned it elsewhere, right? Doubtful. The end result is that most of us don't know much about it, and therefore don't do much about it. Finally, since we were never exposed to or taught about passive income and investing, we have never given it much attention. We have largely based our career and business choices on generating working income. If you understood from an early age that a primary financial goal was to create passive income, wouldn't you reconsider some of those career choices? I'm always recommending to folks choosing or changing their business or career to find a direction where generating streams of passive income is natural and relatively easy. This is especially important today because so many people work in service businesses where they have to be there personally to make money. There's nothing wrong with being in a personal service business, other than that unless you get on your investment horse pretty soon and do exceptionally well, you'll be trapped into working forever. By choosing business opportunities that immediately or eventually produce passive income, you'll have the best of both worlds—working income now and passive income later. Refer back a few paragraphs to review some of the passive business income options we discussed. Unfortunately, almost everyone has a money blueprint that is set for earning working income and against earning passive income. This attitude will be radically changed after you attend the Millionaire Mind Intensive Seminar, where using experiential techniques, we change your money blueprint so that earning a massive passive income is normal and natural for you. Rich people think long-term. They balance their spending on enjoyment today with investing for freedom tomorrow. Poor people think short-term. They run their lives based on immediate gratification. Poor people use the excuse "How can I think about tomorrow when I can barely survive today?" The problem is that, eventually, tomorrow will become today; if you haven't taken care of today's problem, you'll be saying the same thing again tomorrow too. To increase your wealth, you either have to earn more or live on less. I don't see anyone putting a gun to your head telling you the house you have to live in, the kind of car you have to drive, the clothes you have to wear, or the food you have to eat. You have the power to make choices. It's a matter of priorities. Poor people choose now, rich people choose balance. I think about my in-laws. For twenty-five years my wife's parents owned a variety store, a low-end version of a 7-Eleven and a lot smaller. Most of their income came from the sale of cigarettes, candy bars, ice cream bars, gum, and sodas. They didn't even sell lottery tickets in those days. The average sale was less than a dollar. In short, they were in a "penny" business. Still, they saved most of those pennies. The didn't eat out; they didn't buy fancy clothes;

they didn't drive the latest car. They lived comfortably but modestly and eventually paid off their mortgage and even bought half of the plaza the store was located within. At the age of fifty-nine, by saving and investing "pen-nies,"my fatherin-law was able to retire. I hate to be the one to have to tell you this, but for the most part, buying things for immediate gratification is nothing more than a futile attempt to make up for our dissatisfaction in life. More often than not, "spending" money you don't have comes from "expending" emotions you do have. This syndrome is commonly known as retail therapy. Overspending and the need for immediate gratification have little to do with the actual item you're buying, and everything to do with lack of fulfillment in your life. Of course, if overspending isn't coming from your immediate emotions, it arises from your money blueprint. According to Natalie, another of our students, her parents were the ultimate cheapskates! They used coupons for every thing. Her mother had a file box full of coupons all sorted by category. Her father had a fifteen-year-old car that was rusting, and Natalie was embarrassed to be seen in it, especially when her mom picked her up from school. Anytime she got in the car, Natalie prayed that no one was looking. On vacation, her family never stayed in a motel or hotel; they didn't even fly, but drove eleven days across the country and camped the whole way, every year! Everything was "too expensive." The way they acted, Natalie thought her parents were broke. But her dad earned what she believed was a lot of money at the time, $75,000 a year. She was confused. Because she hated their stingy habits, she became the opposite. She wanted everything to be high-class and expensive. When she moved out on her own and started making her own money, she didn't even realize it, but in a flash, she had spent all the money she had, and then some! Natalie had credit cards, membership cards, you name it. She racked up all of them to the point where she couldn't even pay the minimums anymore! That's when she took the Millionaire Mind Intensive Seminar, and she says it saved her life. At the Millionaire Mind Intensive, during the section where we identify your "money personality," Natalie's whole world changed. She recognized why she had been spending all her money. It was a form of resentment toward her parents for being so cheap. It was also to prove to herself and the world that she wasn't cheap. Since the course, with her blueprint changed, Natalie says she no longer has the urge to spend her money in "stupid" ways. Natalie related she was recently walking through a mall and noticed this gorgeous light brown suede and fur coat hanging in the window display of one of her favorite stores. Immediately her mind said,

"That coat would look great on you, especially with your blond hair. You need that; you don't have a really nice, dressy winter coat." So she walked into the store, and as she was trying it on, she noticed the price tag, $400. She had never spent that much on a coat before. Her mind said, "So what, the coat looks gorgeous on you! Get it. You'll make the money up later." This is where she says she discovered how profound the Millionaire Mind Intensive is. Almost as soon as her mind suggested that she buy the coat, her new and more supportive mind "file" came up and said, "You'd be much better off putting that four hundred dollars toward your FFA account! What do you need this coat for? You already have a winter coat that's okay for now." Before she knew it, she was putting the coat on hold until the next day instead of buying it right there in the moment as usual. She never went back to get the coat. Natalie realized that her mental "material gratification" files had been replaced with "financial freedom" files. She wasn't programmed to spend anymore. She now knows it's fine to take the best of what her parents modeled for her and save money, and at the same time, to treat herself to nice things with her play account. Natalie then sent her parents to the course so they could be more balanced as well. She's thrilled to report, they now stay in motels (not hotels yet), they bought a new car, and in learning how to make their money work for them, they've retired as millionaires.

Rich people see every dollar as a "seed" that can be planted to earn a hundred more dollars, which can then be replanted to earn a thousand more dollars. The trick is to get educated. Learn about the investment world. Become familiar with a variety of different investment vehicles and financial instruments, such as real estate, mortgages, stocks, funds, bonds, currency exchange, the whole gamut. Then choose one primary area in which to become an expert. Begin investing in that area and then diversify into more, later. It comes down to this: poor people work hard and spend all their money, which results in their having to work hard forever. Rich people work hard, save, and then invest their money so they never have to work hard again. DECLARATION: Place your hand on your heart and say... "My money works hard for me and makes me more and more money."

Millions of people "think" about getting rich, and thousands and thousands of people do affirmations, visualizations, and meditations for getting rich. I meditate almost every day. Yet I've never sat there meditating or visualizing and had a bag of money drop on my head. I guess I'm just one of those unfortunate ones who actually has to do something to be a success. Affirmations, meditations, and visualizations are all wonderful tools, but as far as I can tell, none of them on its own is going to bring you real money in the real world. In the real world, you have to take real "action" to succeed. Why is action so critical? Let's go back to our Process of Manifestation. Look at thoughts and feelings. Are they part of the inner world or outer world? Inner world. Now look at results. Are they part of the inner or outer world? Outer world. That means action is the "bridge" between the inner world and the outer world.

Action is the "bridge" between the inner world and the outer world. So if action is so important, what prevents us from taking the actions we know we need to take? Fear! Fear, doubt, and worry are among the greatest obstacles, not only to success, but to happiness as well. Therefore, one of the biggest differences between rich people and poor people is that rich people are willing to act in spite of fear. Poor people let fear stop them. Susan Jeffers even wrote a fantastic book about this, entitled Feel the Fear and Do It Anyway. The biggest mistake most people make is waiting for the feeling of fear to subside or disappear before they are willing to act. These people usually wait forever. One of our most popular programs is the Enlightened Warrior Training Camp. In that training, we teach that a true warrior can "tame the cobra of fear." It doesn't say kill the cobra. It doesn't say get rid of the cobra, and it certainly doesn't say run away from the cobra. It says "tame" the cobra.It is not necessary to try to get rid of fear in order to succeed. Because we are creatures of habit, we need to practice acting in spite of fear, in spite of doubt, in spite of worry, in spite of uncertainty, in spite of inconvenience, in spite of discomfort, and even to practice acting when we're not in the mood to act. I remember teaching an evening seminar in Seattle, and near the end, I was letting people know about the upcoming threeday Millionaire Mind Intensive Seminar being held in Vancouver. This one fella stands up and says, "Harv, I've had at least a dozen of my family and friends attend the course, and the results have been absolutely phenomenal. Every one of them is ten times happier than before, and they're all on the road to financial success. They all said it was life changing, and if you were holding the course in Seattle, I'd definitely come too." I thanked him for his testimonial and then asked if he was open to some coaching. He agreed and I said, "I have only three words for you." He cheerfully replied, "What are they?" To which I tersely responded, "You're frickin' broke!" Then I asked him how he was doing financially. He sheepishly replied, "Not too good." Of course I replied, "No kidding." I then began ranting and raving at the front of the room: "If you are going to let a three-hour drive or a threehour flight or a three-day trek stop you from doing something you need and want to do, then what else will stop you? Here's the easy answer: anything! Anything will stop you. Not because of the size of the challenge but because of the size of you! "It's simple," I continued. "Either you are a person who will be stopped, or you are a person who won't be stopped. You choose. If you want to create wealth or any other kind of success, you have to be a warrior. You have to be willing to do whatever it takes. You have to 'train' yourself to not be stopped by anything. "Getting rich is not always convenient. Getting rich is not always easy. In fact, getting rich can be pretty damn hard. But so what? One of the key enlightened warrior principles states, 'If you are willing to do only what's easy, life will be hard. But if you are willing to do what's hard, life will be easy.' Rich people don't base their actions on what's easy and convenient; that way of living is reserved for the poor and most of the middle class." If you are willing to do only what's easy, life will be hard. But if you are willing to do what's hard, life will be easy. The tirade was over. The crowd was silent. Later, the fella who'd started the entire discussion came up and thanked me profusely for "opening his eyes." Of course he registered for the course (even though it was in Vancouver), but what was really funny was overhearing him on the phone as I was leaving, fervently giving the exact same speech I had just given him to one of his friends on the other end of the line. I guess it worked because the next day he called in with three more registrations. They were all from the East Coast... and they were all coming to Vancouver! Now that we've addressed convenience, what about discomfort? Why is acting in spite of discomfort so important? Because "comfortable" is where you're at now. If you want to move to a new level in your life, you must break through your comfort zone and practice doing things that are not comfortable. Let's suppose you are currently leading a level 5 life and you want to move to a level 10 life. Level 5 and below are within your comfort zone, but level 6 and above are outside your box, in your "uncomfort" zone. Meaning, to get to a level 10 life from a level 5 life, you will have to travel through your uncomfort zone. Poor people and most of the middle class are not willing to be uncomfortable. Remember, being comfortable is their biggest priority in life. But let me tell you a secret that only rich and highly successful people know: being comfortable is highly overrated. Being comfortable may make you feel warm, fuzzy, and secure, but it doesn't allow you to grow. To grow as a person you have to expand your comfort zone. The only time you can actually grow is when you are outside your comfort zone. Let me ask you a question. The first time you tried something new, was it comfortable or uncomfortable? Usually uncomfortable. But what happened afterward? The more you did it, the more comfortable it became, right? That's how it goes. Everything is uncomfortable at the beginning, but if you stick with it and continue, you will eventually move through the uncomfort zone and succeed. Then you will have a new, expanded comfort zone, which means you will have become a "bigger" person. Again, the only time you are actually growing is when you are uncomfortable. From now on, whenever you feel uncomfortable, instead of retreating back into your old comfort zone, pat yourself on the back and say, "I must be growing," and continue moving forward.

The only time you are actually growing is when you are uncomfortable. If you want to be rich and successful, you'd better get comfortable with being uncomfortable. Consciously practice going into your uncomfort zone and doing what scares you. Here's an equation I want you to remember for the rest of your life: CZ = WZ. It means your "comfort zone" equals your "wealth zone." By expanding your comfort zone, you will expand the size of your income and wealth zone. The more comfortable you have to be, the fewer risks you will be willing to take, the fewer opportunities you will take advantage of, the fewer people you will meet, and the fewer new strategies you will try. Do you catch my drift? The more comfort becomes your priority, the more contracted you become with fear. On the contrary, when you are willing to s-t-r-e-t-c-h yourself, you expand your opportunity zone, and this allows you to attract and hold more income and wealth. Again, when you have a large "container" (comfort zone), the universe will rush to fill the space. Rich and successful people have a big comfort zone, and they are constantly expanding it to be able to attain and hold more wealth. Nobody ever died of discomfort, yet living in the name of comfort has killed more ideas, more opportunities, more actions, and more growth than everything else combined. Comfort kills! If your goal in life is to be comfortable, I guarantee two things. First, you will never be rich. Second, you will never be happy. Happiness doesn't come from living a lukewarm life, always wondering what could have been. Happiness comes as a result of being in our natural state of growth and living up to our fullest potential. Try this. The next time you are feeling uncomfortable, uncertain, or afraid, instead of shrinking and retreating back to safety, press forward. Notice and experience the feelings of discomfort, recognizing that they are only feelings—and that they do not have the power to stop you. If you doggedly continue in spite of discomfort, you will eventually reach your goal. Whether the feelings of discomfort ever subside doesn't matter. In fact, when they do lessen, take it as a sign to increase your objective, because the minute you get comfortable, you have stopped growing. Again, to grow yourself to your fullest potential, you must always be living at the edge of your box. And because we are creatures of habit, we must practice. I urge you to practice acting in spite of fear, practice acting in spite of inconvenience, practice acting in spite of discomfort, and practice acting even when you're not in the mood.By doing so, you will quickly move to a higher level of life. Along the way, make sure you check your bank account, because, guaranteed, that will be growing quickly too. At this point in some of my evening seminars I ask the audience, "How many of you are willing to practice acting in spite of fear and discomfort?" Usually everyone puts his or her hand up (probably because they're scared to death I'm going to "pick" on them). Then I say, "Talk is cheap! Let's see whether you mean it." I then pull out a wooden arrow with a steel-pointed tip and explain that as a practice for this discipline, you're going to break this arrow with your throat. I then demonstrate how the steel point goes into the soft part of your throat, while another person holds the other end of the arrow against their outstretched palm. The idea is to walk straight into the arrow and break it using only your throat before it pierces through your neck. At this point most people are in shock! Sometimes I pick one volunteer to do this exercise, sometimes I hand out arrows to everyone. I've done audiences where over a thousand people are breaking arrows! Can this feat be accomplished? Yes. Is it scary? You bet. Is it uncomfortable? Absolutely. But again, the idea is that fear and discomfort do not stop you. The idea is to practice, to train yourself to do whatever it takes, and to act in spite of anything that might be in your way. Do most people break the arrow? Yes, everyone who walks into it with 100 percent commitment breaks it. However, those who walk into it slowly, halfheartedly, or not at all, don't. After the arrow exercise I ask people, "How many of you found the arrow easier to break physically than what your mind made it up to be?" All agree it was actually a lot easier than they thought it would be. Why is this so? Here comes one of the most important lessons you will ever learn. Your mind is the greatest soap-opera scriptwriter in history. It makes up incredible stories, usually based in dramas and disasters, of things that never happened and probably never will. Mark Twain said it best: "I've had thousands of problems in my life, most of which never actually happened." One of the most important things you can ever understand is that you are not your mind. You are much bigger and greater than your mind alone. Your mind is a part of you just as your hand is a part of you. Here's a thought-provoking question: What if you had a hand that was just like your mind? It was scattered all over the place, it was always beating you up, and it never shut up. What would you do with it? Most people answer something like "Cut it off !" But your hand is a powerful tool, so why would you cut it off ? The real answer of course is you'd want to control it, manage it, and train it to work for you instead of against you. Training and managing your own mind is the most important skill you could ever own, in terms of both happiness and success, and that's exactly what we've been doing with this book and will continue to do with you should you attend one of our live programs. Training and managing your own mind is the most important skill you could ever own, in terms of both happiness and success. How do you train your mind? You start with observation. Notice how your mind consistently produces thoughts that are not supportive to your wealth and happiness. As you identify those thoughts, you can begin to consciously replace those nonempowering thoughts with empowering ones. Where do you find these empowering ways of thinking? Right here, in this book. Every one of the declarations in this book is an empowering and successful way of thinking. Adopt these ways of thinking, being, and attitudes as your own. You don't have to wait for a formal invitation. Decide right now that your life would be better if you chose to think in the ways we've been describing in this book, instead of through the self-defeating mental habits of the past. Make a decision that from now on, your thoughts do not run you, you run your thoughts. From now on, your mind is not the captain of the ship, you are the captain of the ship, and your mind works for you. You can choose your thoughts. You have the natural ability to cancel any thought that is not supporting you, at any time. You can also install selfempowering thoughts at any time, simply by choosing to focus on them. You have the power to control your mind. As I mentioned earlier, at one of my seminars one of my closest friends and best-selling author Robert Allen said something quite profound: "No thought lives in your head rent-free." What that means is that you will pay for negative thoughts. You will pay in money, in energy, in time, in health, and in your level of happiness. If you want to quickly move to a new level of life, begin dividing your thoughts into one of two categories—empowering or disem- powering. Observe the thoughts you have, and determine if they are supportive to your happiness and success or not supportive. Then choose to entertain only empowering thoughts while refusing to focus on disempowering ones. When a nonsupportive thought bubbles up, say "Cancel" or "Thank you for sharing" and replace it with a more supportive way of thinking. I call this process power thinking, and mark my words, if you practice it, your life will never be the same again. That is a promise! So what is the difference between "power thinking" and "positive" thinking? The distinction is slight but profound. To me, people use positive thinking to pretend that everything is rosy, when they really believe that it's not. With power thinking, we understand that everything is neutral, that nothing has meaning except for the meaning we give it, and that we are going to make up a story and give something its meaning. This is the difference between positive thinking and power thinking. With positive thinking, people believe that their thoughts are true. Power thinking recognizes that our thoughts are not true, but since we're making up a story anyway, we might as well make up a story that supports us. We don't do this because our new thoughts are "true" in an absolute sense, but because they are more useful to us and feel a heck of a lot better than nonsupportive ones. Before we leave this section, I must warn you—do not attempt the arrow-break exercise at home. The exercise has to be set up in a specific way or you could hurt yourself as well as others around you. At our programs we use protective equipment. If you have an interest in these types of breakthrough exercises, see the description of the Enlightened port your happiness and success. Challenge the little voice in your head whenever it tells you "I can't" or "I don't want to" or "I don't feel like it." Don't allow this fear-based, comfortbased voice to get the better of you. Make a pact with yourself that whenever the voice tries to stop you from doing something that would be supportive to your success, you will do it anyway, to show your mind that you are the boss, not it. Not only will you increase your confidence dramatically, but eventually this voice will get quieter and quieter as it recognizes it has little effect on you.

Rich people constantly learn and grow. Poor people think they already know. At the beginning of my live seminars, I introduce people to what I call "the three most dangerous words in the English language." Those words are "I know that." So how do you know if you know something? Simple. If you live it, you know it. Otherwise, you heard about it, you read about it, or you talk about it, but you don't know it. Put bluntly, if you're not really rich and really happy, there's a good chance you still have some things to learn about money, success, and life. As I explained at the beginning of this book, during my "broke" days, I was fortunate to get some advice from a multimillionaire friend who had some compassion for my plight. Remember what he said to me: "Harv, if you're not as successful as you'd like to be, there's something you don't know." Fortunately, I took his suggestion to heart and went from being a "know-it-all" to a "learn-it-all." From that moment on, everything changed. Poor people are often trying to prove that they're right. They put on a mask as if they've got it all figured out, and it's just some stroke of bad luck or a temporary glitch in the universe that has them broke or struggling. One of my more famous lines is "You can be right or you can be rich, but you can't be both." Being "right" means having to hold on to your old ways of thinking and being. Unfortunately, these are the ways that got you exactly where you are now. This philosophy also pertains to happiness, in that "you can be right or you can be happy."

You can be right or you can be rich, but you can't be both. There's a saying that author and speaker Jim Rohn uses that makes perfect sense here: "If you keep doing what you've always done, you'll keep getting what you've always got." You already know "your" way, what you need is to know some new ways. That's why I wrote this book. My goal is to give you some new mental files to add to the ones you already have. New files mean new ways of thinking, new actions, and therefore new results. That's why it's imperative you continue to learn and grow. Physicists agree that nothing in this world is static. Everything alive is constantly changing. Take any plant. If a plant isn't growing, it is dying. It's the same with people as well as all other living organisms: if you are not growing, you are dying. One of my favorite sayings is by author and philosopher Eric Hoffer, who said, "The learners shall inherit the earth while the learned will be beautifully equipped to live in a world that no longer exists." Another way of saying that is, if you're not continuously learning, you will be left behind. Poor people claim they can't afford to get educated due to lack of time or money. On the other hand, rich people relate to Benjamin Franklin's quote: "If you think education is expensive, try ignorance." I'm sure you've heard this before, "knowledge is power," and power is the ability to act. Whenever I offer the Millionaire Mind Intensive program, I find it interesting that it's usually the people who are the most broke who say, "I don't need the course," "I don't have the time," or "I don't have the money." Meanwhile, the millionaires and multimillionaires all register and say, "If I can learn just one new thing or make one improvement, it's worth it." By the way, if you don't have the time to do the things you want to do or need to do, you're most probably a modern slave. And if you don't have the money to learn how to be successful, you probably need it more than anyone. I'm sorry, but saying "I don't have the money" just doesn't cut it. When will you have the money? What is going to be different a year or two years or five years from now? Here's the easy answer: nothing! And you'll be saying the exact same words again at that time. The only way I know for you to have the money you want is to learn how to play the money game inside and out. You need to learn the skills and strategies to accelerate your income, to manage money, and to invest it effectively. The definition of insanity is doing the same thing over and over and expecting different results. Look, if what you've been doing were working, you'd already be rich and happy. Anything else your mind conjures up as a response is nothing more than an excuse or justification. I hate to be so in your face about it, but the way I see it, that's my job. I believe a good coach will always ask more of you than you will ask of yourself. Otherwise, why the heck do you need one? As a coach, my goal is to train you, inspire you, encourage you, coax you, and have you observe, in full living color, what is holding you back. In short, to do whatever it takes to move you to the next level in your life. If I have to, I'll rip you apart and then piece you back together in a way that works. I'll do whatever it takes to make you ten times happier and a hundred times as rich. If you're looking for Pollyanna, I'm not your guy. If you want to move quickly and permanently, let's continue. Success is a learnable skill. You can learn to succeed at anything. If you want to be a great golfer, you can learn how to do it. If you want to be a great piano player, you can learn how to do it. If you want to be truly happy, you can learn how to do it. If you want to be rich, you can learn how to do it. It doesn't matter where you are right now. It doesn't matter where you are starting from. What matters is that you are willing to learn. One of my better-known quotes is "Every master was once a disaster." Here's an example. A while ago, I had an Olympic skier in my seminar. When I made that statement, he stood up and asked to share. He was adamant, and for some reason I thought he was going to vehemently disagree. To the contrary, he told everyone the story of how when he was a kid, he was the worst skier of all his buddies. How they sometimes wouldn't call him to go skiing with them because he was so slow. To fit in, he went to the mountain early each weekend and took lessons. Pretty soon he not only kept up with his buddies, he surpassed them. He then got involved in the racing club and learned from a top-ranked coach. His exact words were "I might be a master skier now, but I definitely started out as a disaster. Harv's absolutely right. You can learn to succeed at anything. I learned how to succeed at skiing, and my next goal is to learn how to succeed with money!" No one comes out of the womb a financial genius. Every rich person learned how to succeed at the money game, and so can you. Remember, your motto is, if they can do it, I can do it! Becoming rich isn't as much about getting rich financially as about whom you have to become, in character and mind, to get rich. I want to share a secret with you that few people know: the fastest way to get rich and stay rich is to work on developing you! The idea is to grow yourself into a "successful" person. Again, your outer world is merely a reflection of your inner world. You are the root; your results are the fruits. There's a saying I like: "You take yourself with you wherever you go." If you grow yourself to become a successful person, in strength of character and mind, you will naturally be successful in anything and everything you do. You will gain the power of absolute choice. You will gain the inner power and ability to choose any job, business, or investment arena and know you'll be a success. This is the essence of this book. When you are a level 5 person, you get level 5 results. But if you can grow into a level 10 person, you will get level 10 results. Heed this warning, however. If you don't do the inner work on yourself, and somehow you make a lot of money, it would most likely be a stroke of luck and there's a good chance you'd lose it. But if you become a successful "person" inside and out, you'll not only make it, you'll keep it, grow it, and most important, you'll be truly happy. Rich people understand the order to success is BE, DO, HAVE. Poor and middle-class people believe the order to success is HAVE, DO, BE.

Poor and most middle-class people believe "If I have a lot of money, then I could do what I want and I'd be a success." Rich people understand, "If I become a successful person, I will be able to do what I need to do to have what I want, including a lot of money." Here's something else only rich people know: the goal of creating wealth is not primarily to have a lot of money, the goal of creating wealth is to help you grow yourself into the best person you can possibly be. In fact, that is the goal of all goals, to grow yourself as a person. World-renowned singer and actress Madonna was asked why she kept changing her persona, her music, and her style every year. She responded that music was her way to express her "self" and that reinventing herself each year forces her to grow into the kind of person she wants to be. In short, success is not a "what," it's a "who." The good news is that "who" you are is totally trainable and learnable. I should know. By no means am I perfect or even close to it, but when I look at who I am today as opposed to who I was twenty years ago, I can see a direct correlation between "me and my wealth" (or lack of it) then and "me and my wealth" now. I learned my way to success and so can you. That's why I'm in the training business. I know from personal experience that virtually any person can be trained to succeed. I was trained to succeed, and now I've been able to train tens of thousands of others to succeed. Training works! I've found that another key difference between rich people and poor and middle-class people is that rich people are experts in their field. Middle-class people are mediocre in their field, and poor people are poor in their field. How good are you at what you do? How good are you at your job? How good are you at your business? Do you want a totally unbiased way of knowing? Look at your paycheck. That will tell you everything. It's simple: to get paid the best, you must be the best.

To get paid the best, you must be the best. We recognize this principle in the professional sports world every day. Generally, the best players in every sport earn the most. They also make the most money on endorsements. This same principle also holds true in both the business and financial worlds. Whether you choose to be a business owner, a professional, a network marketing distributor, whether you're in commissioned sales or a salaried job, whether you're an investor in real estate, stocks, or anything else, all things being equal: the better you are at it, the more you'll earn. This is just another reason why being a continuous learner and enhancing your skill in whatever arena you are in is imperative. On the topic of learning, it's worth noting that rich people not only continue to learn, they make sure they learn from those who have already been where they themselves want to go. One of the things that made the biggest difference for me personally was whom I learned from. I always made it a point to learn from true masters in their respective fields—not those who claimed to be experts, but those who had real-world results to back up their talk. Rich people take advice from people who are richer than they are. Poor people take advice from their friends, who are just as broke as they are. I recently had a meeting with an investment banker who wanted to do business with me. He was suggesting I place several hundred thousand dollars with him to get started. He then asked me to forward him my financial statements so he could make his recommendations. I looked him in the eye and said, "Excuse me, but don't you have this backward? If you want me to hire you to handle my money, wouldn't it be more appropriate for you to forward me your financial statements? And if you're not really rich, don't bother!" The man was in shock. I could tell that no one had ever questioned his own net worth as a stipulation for investing with him. It's absurd. If you were going to climb Mount Everest, would you hire a guide who's never been to the summit before, or would it be smarter to find someone who's made it to the top several times and knows exactly how to do it? So, yes, I am absolutely suggesting you put serious attention and energy into continuously learning and, at the same time, be cautious of whom you are learning and taking advice from. If you learn from those who are broke, even if they're consultants, coaches, or planners, there's only one thing they can teach you—how to be broke! By the way, I highly recommend you consider hiring a personal success coach. A good coach will keep you on track in doing what you've said you want to do. Some coaches are "life" coaches, meaning they handle the gamut of everything, while other coaches have specialties that might include personal or professional performance, finances, business, relationships, health, and even spirituality. Again, find out your prospective coach's background to ensure the coach has demonstrated success in the arenas of importance to you. Just as there are successful paths to climbing Mount Everest, there are proven routes and strategies for creating high income, fast financial freedom, and wealth. You have to be willing to learn them and use them. Again, as part of our Millionaire Mind Money Management method, I strongly suggest that you put 10 percent of your income into an Education Fund. Use this money specifically for courses, books, tapes, CDs, or any other way you choose to educate yourself, whether through the formal education system, private training companies, or personalized, one-onone coaching. Whatever method you choose, this fund ensures you will always have the wherewithal to learn and grow instead of repeating the poor person's refrain of "I already know." The more you learn, the more you earn . . . and you can take that to the bank! DECLARATION: Place your hand on your heart and say... "I am committed to constantly learning and growing."

CHAPTER NINE

Danny Dollar Millionaire Extraordinaire

Danny Dollar, Millionaire Extraordinaire. Yes, you read it right, MILLIONAIRE!!! Ok, I'm not a millionaire yet, but I'm gonna be! Yep, this little knucklehead kid is gonna make it big. Not only will I become a millionaire, I've got a plan to do it by the time I'm 21 years old. That's about 10 years from now. And I'll tell you how I'm gonna do it in one word: INVESTING! That's right, I said investing. Okay, you might be asking yourself, "What the heck is investing?" Well, I'll tell you. But first, a little bit about me. I'm eleven years old, and I live in the Eastchester section of the Bronx, New York, along with my Mom, Dad, and older sister. I'm your typical kid; I love music, I really love basketball, but the thing I love the most is, well, money. Now I know everyone loves money, but not like me. I'm a money maniac. I love money like other kids love candy. I know everything there is to know about money. For example, did you know that the first forms of money were animals, like cows? Yep, cows! People would trade cattle and other animals for things that they wanted. That's called bartering. Bartering is when you trade something you have for something you want. Imagine going to the sneaker store and telling the guy behind the counter: "Yo, I'll give you three cows for these sneakers." "With tax it comes up to three cows and two chickens." Dang!

Danny Dollar Millionaire

That would be crazy! In case you're wondering how I earn the money that I love so much, well DUH, I have a job! Actually, I've got a few jobs. I walk Mrs. Gonzalez's dogs before and after school. Cha-Ching! I go to the store for Mr. Milton every other day; he's kinda old. Cha-Ching! I rake leaves in the fall, shovel snow in the winter, wash cars and mow lawns in the summer, Cha-Ching, Cha-Ching, Cha-Ching! You get the picture. By the end of the week, I'm hauling in about one hundred dollars. That's serious paper for an 11-year-old kid. Every Saturday I'm off to my favorite place in the world, THE BANK! Yep, the bank. The people there are crazy cool. As soon as I walk in, the security guard, Mr. Block, always says, "Dollar Dan, the Man with the plan." And I say, "Mr. Block, got the bank on lock." I really like that dude. Then I go to the same teller, Mrs. Susan Anthony. She always greets me with a "Good morning, Mr. Dollar." Mr. Dollar! Man, do I like the sound of that! I deposit all I've earned throughout the week, except for ten dollars that I keep for playing around with. After Mrs. Anthony updates my bankbook, I give her a little wink, she winks back, and it's a wrap. I'm done. I'm almost floating on the way back home thinking about how much money I've saved. And what I'm saving for is awesome. It's big, it's huge, it's colossal! It's part of my goal to becoming a millionaire. Okay, okay, okay...I'll tell you. You know how some kids want to be a big-time basketball player? Well not me, I want to be a big-time basketball team owner, just like my idol Rocky Austin. Mr. Austin started out flippin' burgers as a kid and now owns a billion dollar fast food chain called "Flippin' Burgers" and he owns the Texas Mustangs basketball team, too. So, now you've got it. I want to own a basketball team. That's my dream! How am I gonna get enough money to own a basketball team? I told you earlier— INVESTING! Here's the plan, so pay attention: investing means taking your money and buying something that will make you more money, like a stock or a bond. With stock, you pay money to a company and then you actually own a small part of that company, for example, the Yola-Cola Company. They make my favorite soft drink. Let's say I own stock in Yola-Cola. When they make a lot of money I get a piece, so the more stock that I own, the bigger the piece I get. If Yola-Cola doesn't make money, I could lose some of the money I've invested. Sounds risky I know, but like my Dad always says, "No risk, no reward." A bond is a little less risky than buying stock. With a bond, you let a business or the government borrow your money and they promise to give that money back with interest. Interest is money they give you for letting them borrow your money. Sometimes, I loan my big-head sister five bucks and I charge her two bucks to borrow my five bucks. When she pays me back, she has to give me seven bucks. I just made two bucks in interest for loaning her only five. Get it?! Sounds cool, right? (Although sometimes she tries to jerk me out of my two bucks, so I hold her diary hostage. HAHA, it works every time). So, I take most of the money that I earn and put it into the bank or invest it into stocks and bonds. The money I earn in interest or by investing, I reinvest into other things. That's called diversifying. Diversifying is when you invest your money into different things to try and make more money. ARE YOU GETTING ALL OF THIS?! I know it's a lot to swallow; you should have seen me trying to explain all this to my parents. Their heads are still spinning. But when they're sitting in the skybox watching my team win a championship, I'm sure they'll say to each other, "That Yola-Cola stock really paid off!" Yep, one day I'm gonna be a millionaire. I'll be a successful Wall Street investor who owns a professional basketball team; who gives to charities and helps those less fortunate; who conquers the global financial industry. I'm gonna achieve all my goals and dreams. But being a future millionaire isn't easy. There's a lot of responsibility that goes with being

"Dan, the Man." Responsibility and sacrifice. Until I become a millionaire, I've got poop to pick up. Let me explain, just the other day, I was playing basketball with the guys when the alarm on my watch went off. It was four o'clock and time for me to walk Mrs. Gonzalez's dogs. We were winning thirty to twenty; the game was intense. The guys begged me not to go, but I made a promise to Mrs. Gonzalez that I would be on time. It was her bingo night and she couldn't be late, so I couldn't be late. That meant leaving before the game was over. I had my friend Noogie take my place playing ball, which did not make the guys on my team happy. They called me a peanut head. Can you believe that?! But I would rather be called a peanut head than be called irresponsible. Because of Noogie, my team lost the game thirty to forty. After I left, they didn't score another point, and they called ME a peanut head?! When I got to Mrs. G's house, those dogs were buggin' out! There are three of them, all Chihuahuas: Nina, Pinta, and Santa Maria. Walking them was a nightmare. First, Nina picked a fight with a huge pit bull. She was barking like that dog owed her money. The funny thing was that the pit bull backed down. You had to see it to believe it. Then, Pinta had an accident on Pablo's new sneakers. Pablo is the neighborhood bully. He was furious and vowed he would get me back. I told him that it wasn't my fault; a dog's gotta do what a dog's gotta do. As I walked away, I shouted, "Pee you later." HAHA! He didn't like that at all. To make things worse, Santa Maria got loose and decided to chase pigeons. Then, the pigeons decided to use her as target practice. Guess who had to give Santa Maria a bath? Yep, peanut head! Did I mention having to pick up their poop? Oh well, it was worth it. Mrs. G. gave me ten bucks for walking her dogs plus a five dollar tip for washing Santa Maria. Chaching! That's fifteen dollars for about one hour of work. Not bad, but that's nothing compared to the money I'll make with the lemonade stand that I've got planned. Chapter 1 Pablo's Woes "Yo Noogie, pass me the ball," Danny yelled. "Try and get it!" teased Noogie. "Alright, that's enough playing around. Let's get a real game going. Come on, two on two. Me and Benjamin against Andrew and Noogie," Danny screamed out. "Why do I always get stuck with Noogie?" asked Andrew. "Cause you both stink!" said Benjamin, as he made a perfect jump shot. The ball sank into the hoop then rolled across the court, where it was picked up by Pablo. Pablo stepped onto the court followed by his boys, Washington and Fingers. He ignored the other boys and passed the ball to Washington, who then passed it to Fingers. "Hey, give us the ball back," yelled Benjamin. "If you want it, come and get it chumps!" Pablo yelled back. Noogie tried to grab the ball and accidentally stepped on Pablo's new sneakers. "YO, ARE YOU CRAZY?! I just paid a hundred dollars for these kicks!" Pablo screamed. "You paid one hundred bucks for a pair of sneakers, you got played!" said Danny. "You're just mad because my sneakers are nicer than yours, and I didn't get played, my Moms bought them for me!" said Pablo. Danny thought to himself, 'Didn't Pablo's mother just get laid off from work. How can she afford to buy those sneakers?' "Let's get outta here and let the girls play their little basketball game," Pablo said, as he threw the ball hard at Andrew. "Man, that dude has a serious attitude problem," said Andrew. "Yeah, he's got issues," Danny responded. --- Later at Pablo's house, Pablo yelled, "Yo, Mom, what's for dinner? I'm starving." "Grilled cheese," his mom replied with a sigh. "Are you kidding me, grilled cheese again? We've had grilled cheese three times this week. Can I at least have two?" "No honey, grilled cheese is all we can afford, and we only have enough for two, one for you and one for me." Pablo thinks to himself as he looks down at the scuff on his new sneakers, 'Man, all my Mom can afford for us to eat are grilled cheese sandwiches. Maybe I shouldn't have begged her to buy me these sneakers.'

CHAPTER TEN

Secrets Of The Millionaire Traders

If you are trading with funds you need for some family project, you are doomed to failure. This is because you won't be able to enjoy the mental freedom to make sound trading decisions, say the millionaire traders. Your trading funds should be viewed as money you are willing to lose. Your position should be carefully analyzed so you don't jeopardize other funds or assets. One of the keys to successful trading is mental independence. "You've got to trade outside influencing factors, and that means your trading freedom must not be influenced by the fear of losing money you really have earmarked for a specific need", said one trader. "The market place is not the arena for scared money", agreed another.

You need an objective temperament, an ability to control emotions and carry a position without losing sleep. Although trading discipline can be developed, the successful traders are unemotional about their position. Click here to learn more about developing discipline and removing emotional trading. Successful traders suggest that people who can't control emotions look elsewhere for profits. "There are many exciting things happening in the market everyday, so it takes a hard-nosed type of attitude and an ability to stand above short-term circumstances. If you do not have this attitude you will be changing your mind and your position every few minutes", noted one of the millionaires.

Test your trading ability by making paper trades. Then begin to trade small. If you are trading emini contracts, trade a single contract. If you are trading commodities trade small lots of 1000 to 3000 bushels of grain at a time. If your broker doesn't allow you to trade in small lots or single contracts, start with something less volatile, e.g. in commodities trade oats. Beginning traders should learn the mechanics of trading before graduating to more volatile contracts.

One rule of thumb is to keep three times the money in your margin account than is needed for that particular position. Reduce your position if necessary to conform to that rule. This rule helps you avoid trading decisions based on the amount of money in your margin account. If you are under-margined you may be forced to liquidate a position early, at a costly loss that could have been avoided.

Don't hope for a move so much that your trade is based on hope. The successful trader is able to isolate his trading from his emotion. Although hope is a great virtue in other areas of life, it can be a real hindrance to a trader." said once trader. When hoping that the market will turn around in their favor, beginners often violate basic trading rules.

Decide upon a basic course of action, then don't let the ups and downs during the day upset your game play. Decisions made during the trading day based upon a price move or a news item are usually disastrous, say the millionaires. Successful traders prefer to formulate a basic opinion before the market opens, then look for the proper time to execute a decision that has been made - apart from the emotion of the current market. When a trader completely changes his direction during the trading day, it can confuse him and may result in generating lots of commissions with little profit.

A trading break helps you take a detached view of the market, and tends to give you a fresh look at yourself and the way you want to trade for the next several weeks. "Sometimes you get so close to the forest you can't see the trees," said one trader. "A break helps me see the market factors in a better perspective."

Secrets Of The Millionaire Traders

Successful traders like breathing room. When everyone seems to be long, they look for a reason to be short. Historically, the public tends to be wrong. Successful traders feel uncomfortable when their position is popular with the buying public, especially small traders. Periodic government reports on the position of traders of various sizes provide "overcrowding" clues. Another clue is "contrary opinion". When most of the advisory services are long, for example, the successful trader gets ready to move to the sideline or to take a short position. Some services give a reading on market sentiment determined by compiling opinions from many advisory services. If 85% of the analysts are bullish, this indicates an overbought situation. If less than 25% are bullish, this indicates an oversold condition.

Don't be influenced in your trading by what someone says, or you will continually change your mind. Once you have formed a basic opinion in the market direction, don't allow yourself to be easily influenced. You can always find someone who can give you what appear to be logical reasons for reversing your position. If you listen to these outside views, you may be tempted to change your mind only to find later that holding your opinion would have been more profitable.

Don't feel that you have to trade every day, or even hold a position every day. The beginning trader is tempted to trade or hold a position every day and this is a costly tendency. The successful traders develop patience and discipline to wait for an opportunity. After they have taken a position and begin to feel uncomfortable, successful traders either reduce the size of the position or liquidate.

Putting in an order to buy or sell at market may show a lack of discipline, according to one successful trader. To avoid violating this rule, he places specific price limit orders. However there are times when he wants to liquidate a position immediately. Then the market order is helpful. Your goal should be to minimize the use of market orders.

If you are trading emini contracts, there are contracts expiring in March, June, September and December. The nearest month is usually the most active contract until the last few days before expiry. If you are trading commodities, trade the contract with the highest volume and open interest. For example with soybeans, November, March and July usually have the highest volume and open interest, depending on the season. Trading these active months should enable you to get in and out easily. A similar caution should be noted for inactive commodities. Low volume commodities are not the markets for beginning traders because it may be difficult to liquidate a position when you want out. A good broker will be able to give you help in this area.

When trading commodities, watch the "families": grains, the meats or the metals. When you spot a wide divergence in a group, it could signal a trading opportunity. For example, if all grains except soybeans were moving higher, the millionaire traders would look for an opportunity to sell soybeans as soon as the grains in general appeared to be weakening. The reverse of this is true also. The traders would buy the strongest commodity in the group during periods of weakness.

You'll hurt yourself if you try to have the necessary information and "feel" of several different markets, e.g. both stock and futures markets. Know your limitations and trade within these limits. Few traders successfully trade multiple markets at the same time, because they are moved by independent factors.

This is a good price-direction clue, particularly after a major report. A break out of the opening range may tell you the direction of trading for the day or the next several days. If the market breaks through the opening range on the high side, go long. If it breaks out on the bottom side of the opening range, go short.Trade the opening range breakout.

It means never buy until the price trades above the previous days close, or never sell until the price trades below the previous day's close. Followers of a "market momentum philosophy" use this rule. They believe that the weight in the market is in their favor when they wait for trading to break out of the previous day's trading range before adding to their position.

The longer the period you're watching, the more the market momentum behind your decision. So monthly price breakouts are an even stronger clue to price trends and are vitally important for the position trader or hedger. When the price breaks out on the topside of the previous monthly high, it's a buy signal. When the break out is on the bottom side of a previous monthly low, it's a sell signal.

When you add to a position, don't add more contracts at any one time than the number of contracts you already have open. For example if you're trading emini, let's assume your initial position was 4 contracts. An ideal situation would be to pyramid by adding 3 contracts then 2 contracts, then 1 contract, providing the market is moving your way. Try to avoid the "inverted pyramid" type of trading where at each addition you add more than your original position. This is a dangerous trading technique because a minor market reversal can wipe out your profit for the entire position. Your average price is closer to market price in the "inverted pyramid" situation, which makes you vulnerable. Another danger in pyramiding is that of over-committing yourself to the point where you lack sufficient margin money.

If you want to be long a certain number of contracts, or a certain number of shares, you may want to do it 4 or more installments, to see if the market is moving in your direction before you become totally committed. Successful traders use the fundamentals and various technical signals to guide their trading, but the most important key is market action. The millionaire traders tend to wait for the market to verify that the initial position was a good one before putting on their full position

When the market moves against you, admit your mistake by liquidating your position. You can be successful if you are right on less than 50% of your trades if you keep your losses short and let your profits run. Some successful traders have only three or four profitable trades out of ten because through discipline or stop-loss orders they get out early when they are wrong. One of the most common failures of new traders is their inability to admit they're wrong say millionaire traders. It takes a great deal of discipline to overcome the temptation to hang on to a loss, hoping that the market will turn in your favor.

The slogan "you never go broke taking a profit" doesn't apply. The reason: Your losses will at the best cancel out or at worst outweigh your profits unless you let your profits run. How do you know when to take a profit? Some technical rules on reversals and other chart formations can help. The millionaire traders say you should never take a profit just for the sake of a profit - have a reason to close out a profitable position.

One successful trader says: "Learn to like losses because they're part of the business. When you gain the emotional stability to accept a loss without it hurting your pride, you're on your way to becoming a successful trader." The fear of taking a loss must be removed before you become a good trader.

About Author

Arvind is leading **business coach and strategist** for top business owners and entrepreneurs who want to grow their business, life and success. Grow your business to grow your health, wealth and happiness with leading business coach. He is recognised by the University of Pennsylvania top leadership and business expert .

ARVIND UPADHYAY INDIA'S MOST LOVED AUTHOR

Milton Keynes UK
Ingram Content Group UK Ltd.
UKHW021048021124
450589UK00013B/1083

9 798885 697279